Defining Moments

MODERN
W A R

DEFINING MOMENTS

MODERN
W A R

Jonathan Forty

Grange
BOOKS

Published 2005 by Grange Books
an imprint of Grange Books PLC.
The Grange
Kings North Industrial Estate
Hoo nr. Rochester
Kent, UK
ME3 9ND

www.grangebooks.co.uk

All enquiries please email info@grangebooks.co.uk

All notations of errors or omissions and other correspondence (author inquiries,
permissions) concerning the content of this book should be addressed to:
TAJ Books, 27 Ferndown Gardens, Cobham, Surrey, UK, KT11 2BH,
info@tajbooks.com.

ISBN 1-84013-756-8

Printed in China
1 2 3 4 5 09 08 07 06 05

CONTENTS

Introduction

Modern warfare has developed so radically and so fast that combatants from earlier eras would find difficulty in drawing any parallels between their experience of conflict and that of modern times. Modern death can come raining out of clear blue skies sent by the push of a button thousands of miles away. In its ultimate state, battle has become sanitized and emotionally remote for many of the protagonists—but on the ground for the common soldier war is every bit as dirty and dangerous as it ever was no matter what technology is used to dispatch the enemy.

This book looks at modern wars around the globe since World War II and on into the new millennium. World War II was a truly global conflict and its far-reaching effects are still felt today. In many ways the most apparent of these is in the way that technology and science developed, spurred on by the need for new weapons and other wartime requirements. The biggest of these was the development of the atomic bomb: after the war true power was held by those countries which had the bomb. Others with ambition tried to develop the technology so they too could join the "Arms Race" and call the shots. The world was poised on the edge of terrible and instant destruction—amazingly it never happened.

October 28th 1961 Soviet Tanks at the Checkpoint Charlie. Berlin.

November 6, 1962: Soviet personnel and six missile transporters loading onto ship transport at Casilda port. (Note shadow at lower right of RF-101 reconnaissance jet taking the photograph.)

Today's world expects and uses levels of technology that exceed anything that could have been imagined by most people in the 1930s. One of the biggest changes has been in the rapid development of transport technologies so that massive numbers of people and goods can be transported around the globe by air. Also the development of space rocketry and satellites led to remarkable developments in the field of communications, and huge strides in medical science in such fields as disease control, mass immunization, blood serum technology, and plastic surgery.

The only Suez airfield in Allied hands is at El Gamel, where British airborne troops made a landing during the first assault.

US Marines drive down a street in Santo Domingo during the occupation of the Dominican Republic in 1965.

Less immediately memorable from over 60 years' distance and global immediacy are the local political issues that surfaced in the postwar years—although the main reason for this is not just time but because the events were subsumed within the politically electric era known as the Cold War. As soon as the conflict against fascism was resolved in 1948, the world coalesced into two huge alliances that encompassed the entire globe and the space around it. The world was divided into the "free" west represented by the United States of America and the "repressive" east behind the Iron Curtain of the Soviet Union and Communist China. However, the massive ideological rift between the winning allies and the USSR was apparent well before the war ended. The struggle between western capitalism and Soviet communism took place against the terrifying backdrop of the fear of nuclear meltdown created at Hiroshima and Nagasaki in the final days of the war.

Prague residents carrying Czechoslovak flag and throwing burning torches attempt to stop a Soviet tank in downtown Prague.

The first major attack on Soviet held Kabul by mujahideen belonging to Mahaz-e-Melli.

The Armageddon scenario—MAD, mutually assured destruction—meant that the conflict between the two sides, except for the odd close shave, was fought through proxies. Both east and west took sides in every dispute, point of contention, territory, and conflict, pumping in money and weapons—often, we can see now, to the wrong people and in a way that intensified and prolonged conflicts.

While the ideological divide of the Cold War contributed to the battles and wars of the post-World War II period, it did not often cause them—indeed, in the case of the Balkans it could be said to have kept the lid on the pressure cooker allowing 50 years of peace. The main political impetus of the postwar world was decolonization as the once all dominating political powers (Britain, France, Portugal, Spain, etc) relinquished control of lands beyond their borders: sometimes willingly letting them go, but others emphatically not. The battles fought by national movements against colonial powers—followed by civil wars as the winners worked out the internal politics of the country or area in question, often involving centuries-old religious, racial, ethnic, and political tensions, proved every bit as bloody and savage as the larger international conflicts. Such civil wars proved too tempting for the superpowers that almost without exception jumped in to join sides regardless of the justice of the cause.

Huge columns of smoke pour from the wreckage of three multimillion dollar international airlines destroyed by Palestine Liberation Organization guerillas at Dawson's Field in the Jordan desert. The planes, a BOAC VC10, a Swissair passenger airplane and TWA Boeing 707 were hijacked by the PLO during the preceding week.

A definition of terror is perhaps that those who choose to use it will do so by any and all means and see no boundaries, borders, nor innocents. The perennial problem of one man's freedom fighter being another man's terrorist was never truer than in the postwar period when historic grievances could be sorted out without colonial intervention.

A Palestinian guerilla wearing a mask over his face crosses two daggers at a Hamas rally in Gaza.

Shiite militiamen fire rocket propelled grenades into Sabra, a Palestinian refugee camp in Beirut, Lebanon. From 1985 to 1988, Palestinian refugee camps in Lebanon suffered from three separated sieges by the Amal movement, a group of Shiites attempting to keep the PLO from rising to power within Lebanon.

Soldiers escort two members of shining path guerrillas arrested in Lima, Peru.

Khmer Rouge leader Pol Pot talking to a journalist reportedly on in the guerrilla's jungle hide-out in Northern Cambodia. Khmer Rouge cadres and the Thai military said 16 April that Pol Pot has died of a heart attack. Pol Pot is blamed for presiding over the deaths of nearly two million Cambodians.

States are supposed to declare their intentions and obey certain protocols in time of war, most notably the Geneva Convention. In modern times it has become harder to hide atrocities thanks to the proliferation of film, video, television, and most recently, the internet. Control of the media has become crucial, conflict always was a "hearts and minds" operation, but the use and manipulation of images that can be beamed around the world in seconds and into private lives through radio, TV, and the web have become a power too equal to any bomb. Public perception of rights and wrongs is all important and control of these media is true modern power.

In the end all the semantics that describe different kinds of philosophy or approach, and all the -ists and the -isms that are used to mask political aims amount to the same truth: someone trying to control someone else via dogma. Future conflicts will be over exactly the same things as the current and past ones: trade, religion, race, resources, politics, ambition, greed, hatred, wealth, jealousy, rage, revenge, and love. In less than ten thousand years between the use of flint and nuclear weapons the world has changed beyond recognition, but people's desires, hopes, and emotions are basically the same.

A Russian soldier fires from the heavy machine-gun atop his tank, 14 April, during fights with Chechen rebels near Shali. Russian warplanes pounded several villages in southeastern Chechnya overnight Sunday and early Monday despite a unilateral ceasefire declared by Moscow on March 31.

A Tomahawk cruise missile is launched from the USS Philippine Sea (CG 58) in a strike against al Qaeda terrorist training camps and military installations of the Taliban regime in Afghanistan on Oct. 7, 2001.

General Marshall's China Mission efforts to mediate the civil war between Nationalist and Communist forces was abandoned by December 1946. In his final report to the president, Marshall charged both reactionaries in the Kuomintang and hard-liners in the Communist camp with preventing a compromise.

1927-49

The roots of the Chinese Civil War can be traced back to 1912, with the sloughing off of the last vestiges of the ancient and corrupt Imperial Chin regime that had turned its back on the rest of the world and outlived its time. A new style republic was then declared, with Marshal Yuan Shih-k'ai as president, but his death in 1916 saw central government break down and the warlords thrive again.

By 1925 the Chinese Nationalist Party, or Kuomintang (KMT), founded by the respected Dr. Sun Yat-sen, had become the dominant political force; within this party was a political spectrum that included a communist element, soon to become the Chinese Communist Party (CCP). From the upheaval following Sun Yat-sen's death in 1925, Chiang Kai-shek emerged as Chairman of the KMT the following year. In 1927 the communists, led by Mao Tse-tung, rebelled against Chiang Kai-shek's leadership and fled into the mountains of western Kiangsi, beginning the civil war in earnest. Over the next ten years the KMT failed to eradicate the nascent CCP, and so began to lose its dominant position, a process exacerbated by its own corruption and intrigue.

In 1937 outside events intervened when Japan, having occupied Inner Mongolia since 1933, launched a full-scale invasion of China. In the vicious war that ensued, the KMT and CCP declared an uneasy truce

Chiang Kai-shek & May-ling Soong. Chiang Kai-shek died during his fifth term, in 1975. Following her husband's death, Madame Chiang returned to the U.S., residing in Lattington, NY.

until the time that the country had been liberated: the truce allowed the CCP to consolidate its position in northern China.

Following the defeat of Japan in 1945 and the failure of the Chunking Conference, civil war broke out again even more fiercely than before. In 1946 a KMT campaign northward won many battles and gained much territory, but the CCP had come of age. It had built a firm populist power base with a credo that ideally suited the predominantly rural population: in spite of extensive American backing, the KMT could not prevail. Defending such a large area, the Nationalists were spread thin and smaller units could be surrounded and engulfed.

As their forces grew, the CCP inflicted massive losses on the KMT—in 1949 alone, the final year of the civil war, over a million and a half men. No army could sustain such attrition and the Nationalist force swiftly disintegrated. On October 1, 1949, even before outright victory, Mao Tse-tung declared the establishment of the People's Republic of China. On October 13, the Nationalist government fled to Chungking, and by the end of the year the remains of the KMT were forced across the sea to Formosa, now called Taiwan. Here they were ignored by the mainland communist government—primarily because of western pressure and the threat of U.S. retaliation. This remains the position today.

List of participants:... Communist Party (CCP) and Kuomintang (KMT)
Duration: 1927–49
Location: .... China
Outcome: .... CCP victorious: Kuomintang forced to Taiwan
Casualty figures: .... 4–5 million

Ze'ev Jabotinsky founded the Betar youth movement and the Revisionist movement. He was the political leader of the Irgun Zvai Leumi in Eretz Israel.

1944–48

During World War I British troops had fought against the Turks (who were allied to Germany) in the Middle East, most of which was a part of the ailing Ottoman Empire. In 1917 the British entered Palestine and the Balfour Declaration promised support for a Jewish homeland there, provided that "nothing shall be done which may prejudice the civil and religious rights of existing non-Jewish communities in Palestine." The Palestinian Arabs immediately rejected this proposal outright, and so began the first violence between Arab and Jew—which goes on even to this day.

In 1920, Palestine became a British Mandated Territory and Britain tried to police the worsening situation, with its troops becoming increasingly a major target in the process. Ranged against them on the Jewish side was a spectrum of elements, organized partly as a defense against increasing Arab attacks and partly to militate against the British for a Zionist state. The Jewish settlers had formed a self-defense group originally called Hashomar, but with the advent of the British Mandate it became the Haganah. With a membership of 60,000, the Haganah could field an army of 16,000 trained men and also had a full-time force called the Palmach, numbering about 6,000. The more extreme Irgun Zvai Leumi included between 3,000 and 5,000 armed terrorists; it had seceded from the Haganah and Palmach in 1933, for both were ultimately controlled by the Jewish Agency which was in dialogue with the British. Irgun interpreted as compromising with the enemy.

In 1939, one of Irgun's commanding officers, Abraham Stern, in turn

Ben Gurion, Prime Minister of Israel, arriving at London Airport for an informal visit.

left Irgun and formed the still more hardcore Stern Gang, numbering some 200 to 300 fanatics, who began to escalate their terrorist actions against both Palestinians and British. (Stern was killed in a shoot out in Tel Aviv in 1942.) With the beginning of World War II, these actions were mainly suspended, but broke out again with renewed ferocity in 1946, including the bombing of the King David Hotel in Jerusalem, center of the British civilian administration, that killed or injured over 200 people. In November 1947 the United Nations approved a plan to partition Palestine between the Jews and the Arabs—but this was completely rejected by the Palestinians and the Arab League, who stepped up their attacks against Jews. This, in turn, triggered a rising tide of attacks by Jewish terrorists, with hotels, houses, buses, markets, mosques, entire villages, and civilians all considered and treated as legitimate targets. Over the next year the number of Palestinians uprooted from their homes and forced to flee to refugee camps on Israel's borders rose to 300,000.

On March 14, 1948, the State of Israel was proclaimed; on May 15, Britain announced the end of the mandate and began to withdraw. As British forces left, the Arab states invaded and the first Arab-Israeli War started.

List of participants:... Haganah, Palmach, Irgun, Stern Gang, British, Palestinians
Duration:................. 1944–48
Location:.................. Israel, Palestine
Outcome:.................. Israeli independence
Casualty figures: .... 300 British and unknown number of Palestinians killed by Jewish terrorists

Map circulated in the 'Socialist Republic of Macedonia', which includes Thessaloniki in the area of Macedonia claimed by it, 1946.

1944–49

The origins of the Greek Civil War began just before World War II, its fault lines reflecting the concerns of contemporary 20th century political divisions within the country. On one side were the Nationalists/Monarchists (EAM); on the other the communists (KKE) with their military wing, the People's National Army of Liberation (ELAS). At the beginning of World War II Greece declared itself neutral, but it was soon drawn into the conflict by a surprise attack in 1940 by the Italian dictator Mussolini, who had already invaded and occupied Albania in 1939. The Greeks united against the common enemy and fought stubbornly, driving the Italians back into Albania and unwittingly triggering a German invasion through Bulgaria into Macedonia (April 1941)—Hitler not so much aiding the inept Mussolini as protecting the southern flank of his forthcoming invasion of Russia.

Briefly, Greece became a focal point of the global conflict, with increasing numbers of both Allied and Axis troops involved. With the fall of Crete in May 1941, Greece came under Axis control, although resistance continued—despite savage reprisals to the civilian population—with guerrilla bands (the Antartes) supplied by the Allies. Under this pressure the original political fault lines began to reopen among the Greeks, and despite British attempts to mediate, they were often fighting each other as much as the Germans, with ELAS eventually emerging as the more cohesive group. Following the German withdrawal in 1944, ELAS prepared to take over the country but was defeated, after fierce fighting in Athens and Piraeus, by British troops allied to EAM, who then restored the former government to power. In September 1945, the monarchy was restored by plebiscite and King George II returned to Greece.

Greek guerrillas (Antartes).

However, the war was not over yet, for the Greek government was still very unstable and Greece also had unresolved territorial conflicts with Yugoslavia, Bulgaria, and Albania. These states now supported the KKE, whose military wing—ELAS—was renamed the Democratic Army of Greece (DSE). The DSE quickly seized control of a major part of northern Greece, while fighting broke out all over the country and was fiercest in the Vardos Valley. To stabilize the situation Britain sent 40,000 troops and money to the government, which became dependent on this military and financial assistance to stay in power. British military support remained until after the elections of March 31, 1947, and thereafter the burden was taken up by the U.S., with President Truman asking Congress for $400 million of aid for Greece and Turkey. In response, the KKE announced the formation of a communist government and with an army of 20,000–30,000 guerrillas, fought its way south, almost to Athens. Another timely injection of financial and military resources— American—once again stabilized the Greek Government and helped force the communists back to the north. Furthermore, in July 1948 an ideological and personal split between Stalin and Tito brought to an end Yugoslav support for the KKE, who remained loyal to Stalin. This was the real turning point for the rebels. Cut off from regular resupply, their last significant refuge was captured by Government forces on August 28, 1949. This was followed by a formal surrender and an end to the civil war on October 16.

List of participants:	Nationalists/Monarchists (EAM); Communists (KKE)/ (ELAS)
Duration:	1944–49
Location:	Greece
Outcome:	Communists defeated
Casualty figures:	160,000

Boys from West Berlin standing on a heap of rubble wave cheeringly to a US cargo plane that brings food to West Berlin, 1948.

1945–91

By the end of World War II two new global superpowers had emerged and had begun to square up against each other. They espoused the two great political and philosophical theories of the 20th century and fought an ideological war about the way society should be governed—through capitalism or communism.

The geographical power bloc split into the United States, her own possessions, the western European nations and their colonies and commonwealth around the globe. The Union of Socialist and Soviet Republics had its eastern European heartland from whence its ideological mission was to export its political system until all the world shared it. The battleground was the entire globe—land, sea, sky—and even in space above.

The technological development of warfare had received a tremendous boost during five years of continuous struggle, and had culminated in the introduction and use of nuclear weapons, followed soon thereafter by increasingly sophisticated satellite tracking and communication systems. These weapons had such devastating ramifications that when both sides possessed enough of them to promise Mutually Assured Destruction (MAD), it was realized that they couldn't be used. The war, therefore, was "cold"—as in not nuclear—but it was, nevertheless, still very warm indeed in the more conventional means of conflict—bombs, blood, and bullets. For the two superpowers contested all continents, competing for spheres of influence and fighting relentlessly through proxies, automatically backing the opponent's enemy even across the ideological divide.

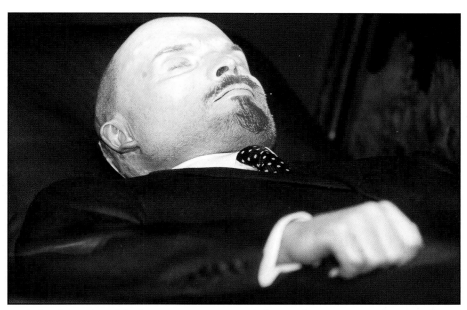

Embalmed founder of the former Soviet Union, Vladimir Ulianov Lenin in his mausoleum in Moscow.

In Europe, the end of the war saw defeated Germany divided into four zones, controlled by the four largest of the Allied powers—the U.S., USSR, UK, and France. Berlin—the old German capital—was in the Soviet sector, and it was here that tension between east and west was first manifested.

With hindsight it is easy to suggest that Stalin's policy—to prevent the reunification of Germany and create instead a zone of client states to act as a buffer against western incursions—was ultimately an unnecessary burden for the USSR. The impoverished client states were a massive drain on resources and also came to resent Soviet tyranny, but the power of the USSR was overwhelming. So, in June 1948 the Soviet Union attempted to prevent a West German state being formed by sealing off Berlin. The western allies launched the Berlin Airlift to keep the city supplied by air for almost a year until May 1949 when the Russians lifted the blockade.

Between 1945 and 1961 approximately three million people fled from East Germany to the west, the main route of departure being through Berlin. In order to stem this flow, in August 1961 the East German Government sealed off access to West Berlin by erecting a barbed-wire fence that later was replaced by a concrete wall—ostensibly to keep

List of participants:... U.S. and NATO, USSR and Warsaw Pact
Duration:................. 1945–91
Location: .... World-wide
Outcome:................. Dissolution of the USSR
Casualty figures: .... Unknown

This archive photo from October 28th 1961 shows Soviet Tanks at the Checkpoint Charlie sector crossing point for diplomats and foreigns in the Friederichstrasse. It was taken just a few days after American tanks had taken up position on the opposite side.

invaders out, but in reality to keep their own populations prisoner. All attempts to rebel or change in the east were viciously suppressed. The Berlin Wall was the physical manifestation of what Winston Churchill called the "Iron Curtain," a border between east and west Europe that separated the two ideologies with a massive military barrier, behind which both sides practiced the final scenario—which was indefinitely delayed yet always imminent.

They grouped together under alliances: NATO—the North Atlantic Treaty Organization—was founded in 1949 and consisted of the United States, most western European nations, and Canada. This was balanced by the Warsaw Pact—a similar grouping of communist countries led by the Soviet Union. With this stalemate the Cold War moved on, first to Asia, then the Caribbean, and the Middle East. It would become a protracted 40-year struggle, testing the stamina of both superpowers' economic, social, and political systems. On smaller battlefields and in different theaters, both sides fueled and armed local rivalries with hardware.

   The threat of nuclear war saw the U.S. and the USSR begin
negotiations on the reduction or limitation of their nuclear capability.
The Strategic Arms Limitation Talks in the late 1960s and 1970s
eventually led to the signing of the SALT accords in 1972 by Nixon
and Brezhnev. SALT I limited each country's ballistic missile defense
and froze the deployment of intercontinental ballistic missile (ICBM)
launchers. SALT II signed by Carter and Brezhnev in 1979, set limits on
the number of strategic missile launchers and other systems each country
could deploy. Both countries largely followed these agreements and a
scaling-down process began, marking a beginning of the end of the Cold
War, which could be said to have finished with the break up of the USSR
in 1991.

Nikita Krushchev(left) and Marshal Nikolai Bulganin.

Ramstein, Germany: 78-years-old Berlin Airlift veteran, retired USAF Colonel Gail S. Halvorsen from Spanish Folk/Utah, gives a thumbs-up as he stands in front of a "Hercules" transport aircraft on Ramstein Air Force Base, he became famous as "Candy-Bomber" during the Berlin blockade some 50 years ago and was a honorary guest during the recent Airlift commemoration ceremonies in Berlin.

*Thousands attend the unveiling of the Airlift Monument (Luftbrueckendenkmal) in front of the airport Tempelhof in Berlin, 10 July 1951. *...The monument is dedicated to the airlift, which was organized during the Berlin blockade in 1948 and 1949. When the Soviets blocked all traffic to and from the Western sectors, which were enclosed by the Soviet Zone, the Western Powers organized an airlift to supply West Berlin with food via the so-called Candy Bombers. The Mayor of Berlin during the unveiling described the monument as a memorial of peace and the cooperation of free people.*

'Manny' Shinwell, later Lord Shinwell, then War Secretary, sees off 1,500 officers and men of the 2nd Guards Brigade from Ocean Dock in Southampton, on their way to Malaya in the 'Empire Trooper'.

1948–60

During World War II, the Japanese occupied Malaya, treating the Malays leniently, but their arch enemies the Chinese with customary brutality. As a result many Chinese fled into the jungle to join the communist-inspired Malayan People's Anti-Japanese Army (MPAJA), which was actively supported by the British. At the end of that war, the British brokered constitutional and federation agreements between Malay, Chinese, and Indian leaders. The Malayan Communist Party (MCP), having lost the initiative to more traditional and conservative forces, remobilized the MPAJA under the new name of the Malayan Races Liberation Army (MRLA), and began a campaign to undermine the government. A state of emergency was declared on June 16, 1948, following the murder of three European rubber estate managers, with the government forces fielding 11 British infantry battalions—22,500 troops—as well as loyal native forces. The MRLA's forces consisted of some 10,000 jungle-based militia.

The communists stepped up their terror campaign, ambushing the security forces, sabotaging installations, derailing trains, bombing buses, as well as torturing and murdering both British and native men, women, and children. By April 1950 there had been such an escalation in terrorist numbers and incidents that the number of British troops was doubled and Lt-Gen Sir Harold Briggs was appointed director of operations to implement his "Briggs Plan." This consisted of resettling nearly 500,000 of the Chinese rural population in strongly protected "new villages" to separate them from contact with the guerrillas, who relied upon them for support and information. Another important factor in the equation was the battle for the "hearts and minds" of the people. When they were resettled, they were given identity cards. This enfranchised them as genuine participants in Malayan society and meant that they would not

High Commissioner General Sir Gerald Templer.

remain landless shanty-town dwellers on the fringes.

The MRLA lacked the support of the whole population, for the Muslim Malays were opposed to communism and also wary of domination by the Chinese. This resulted in the Malay Police and Special Forces giving strong support to the British. In February 1952, Gen Sir Gerald Templer was appointed high commissioner and director of operations; under his dynamic leadership the Briggs Plan was brought to fruition, the tide turned, and the terrorists thereafter were on the run. On August 31, 1957, Malaysia became an independent country within the British Commonwealth, another important factor that removed any justification for an armed insurrection.

By 1960 the previously large terrorist jungle army had been defeated and reduced to a few hundred men near the Thai border. The state of emergency was formally declared to be over on July 31, 1960. It is not clear why the British called the war an "Emergency." One theory is that it was done to hide the seriousness of the situation and constrain its political implications. Another, so that insurance—which would not cover wartime activities—could be claimed on damaged or destroyed property.

List of participants:	MRLA, Britain
Duration:	1948–60
Location:	Malaya
Outcome:	Defeat of the MRLA
Casualty figures:	13,000

This undated archive picture from the early 1950s shows Jordanian field marshal Habees Majali who commanded the fourth Jordanian army battalion in the 1948 Arab-Israeli war.

JUNE 1948–JANUARY 1949

During the final months of the British Mandate in Palestine, the bitter fighting between Arabs and Jews continued to escalate, with fighters drawn from many neighboring Arab countries opposed to the creation of a Jewish state in Palestine. In April 1948 two Jewish groups, Irgun and the Stern Gang, stormed the Arab village of Deir Yasin, massacring 250 people, including women and children. The event struck terror among the Arabs, and triggered an exodus of 300,000 from Palestine. In retaliation an Arab force ambushed and wiped out a Jewish medical convoy. This set the tone of the bitter struggle ahead. Following the declaration of the State of Israel in June 1948, the Arab countries around the new state immediately declared outright war and the armies of six nations: Egypt, Syria, Jordan, Lebanon, Iraq, and Saudi Arabia promptly invaded on four separate fronts.

All were ultimately held and defeated piecemeal and driven back over their own borders by a Jewish army that had been drawn from those with the experience of fighting in other armies all over the world during World War II. Having lived in Europe and the U.S. they had a much better background in the technology of war, coupled with a sense of their own particular religious mission—for an ancient Zionist state to be reborn. The Arabs were united by religion but not by tribe or country, and the single Arab umma ("nation") had been a myth from the beginning, for Egypt, Syria, and Jordan all harbored dreams of being the leader of the pack. The British-trained Arab Legion provided the most difficult opposition to the Israelis, proving that the Arabs did not lack bravery, but leadership.

Efforts by the UN to halt the fighting were unsuccessful until June 11, when a four-week truce was declared. However when the Arab states

The Irgun was a military group that refused to bow to political pressures in securing a state for the Jewish people. Much of the modern Israeli politics today stem from the Irgun and the organization from which they broke, the Hagganah.

refused to renew the truce, the fighting dragged on for ten more days, in which time Israel made more gains and broke the siege of Jerusalem. Fighting on a smaller scale continued during the second UN truce beginning in mid-July, with Israel acquiring substantially more territory, especially in Galilee and the Negev. By January 1949, when the last battles ended, the Jewish state had grown 1,930sq miles beyond the land allocated to it in the UN partition resolution. It had also secured its independence.

The General Armistice Agreements (GAA) were signed on the island of Rhodes between Israel and its Arab opponents—Egypt, Jordan, Lebanon, and Syria—between January and July 1949 under UN supervision. Egypt was left in administrative control of Gaza city and its environs, and the Gaza strip was created. Gazans were not permitted to become Egyptian citizens, nor was the territory ever formally incorporated into Egypt. The ambiguous terms of the GAA paved the way for future Arab-Israeli wars, for the Arabs claimed the right to renew hostilities at any time and steadfastly refused to recognize Israel.

The armistice frontiers remained the de facto boundaries until 1967. 760,000 Palestinians became refugees in surrounding Arab countries as a result of the 1948 war, their status a very significant factor in the Arab-Israeli conflict.

List of participants:... Egypt, Syria, Jordan, Lebanon, Iraq, Saudi Arabia, Israel
Duration:................ June 1948–January 1949
Location:................ Israel/Palestine
Outcome:................ Israel defeats the Arabs
Casualty figures: 20,000

This 18 July, 1950 photo shows men of the US Army 24th Infantry Regiment loaded on trucks for transport up to the firing line during the Korean War.

1950–53

The close of the 19th century saw both Japan and Russia jockeying for control of Korea, with Russia endeavoring to supplant Japanese influence. The Russo-Japanese war (1904–05) followed, with Korea a key prize that ended up under Japanese control. It would remain so until the end of World War II. When Japan surrendered, the Japanese troops in Korea gave themselves up to the Red Army north of the 38th Parallel, and to the U.S. Army south of that line. Two new countries were thereby created: the communist Democratic People's Republic and the Republic of South Korea, and it was here in 1950 that the Cold War next warmed up.

On June 25 the North Korean People's Army (NKPA) invaded South Korea and quickly overran most of the country, capturing the capital Seoul. It pushed the tiny South Korean Army and the small number of U.S. troops, who had swiftly reinforced them from Japan, back into a small perimeter around the southernmost port of Pusan. South Korea turned to the United Nations Organization for help, which was supported by 53 UN member states, of which 17 eventually sent troops to fight in Korea.

Throughout August and September the North Koreans tried to take Pusan, but General Walton Walker, commander of U.S. Eighth Army, not only held off all assaults but also prepared a counterattack. This

United States infantry move to the front line as civilians, caught in the fighting between United Nations forces and North Korean invaders, evacuate their homes and move to a place of safety. One of the women carries her baby on her back.

included a boldly conceived (by General MacArthur) and brilliantly executed amphibious landing at Inchon on September 15, 1950, which led directly to the recapture of Seoul. On September 16, in coordination with the landings, Eighth Army launched an all-out offensive, broke out of Pusan, linked up with the landing forces, and drove the enemy out of South Korea. The UN then sanctioned their forces to follow up and destroy the North Korean Army, even though the Chinese warned they would take action. Capturing the capital Pyongyang, the UN forces pushed on northward toward the Yalu River, convinced that the Chinese were bluffing—but they were not.

List of participants:... U.S., International UN forces, North and South Korea, China
Duration:................. 1950–53
Location:.................. Korea
Outcome:................. Stalemate
Casualty figures: 1,500,000

*Compatriots worlds apart are these Korean soldiers pictured in the South Korean battle zone. The South Korean on the left is guarding two North Koreans captured on a northern sector of the front and brought to a forward command post. * 20/4/01: British veterans of the war and the Duke of York were marking the 50th anniversary of a desperate battle in which 650 British soldiers fought up to 10,000 Chinese troops. Of the 650 soldiers in the 1st Battalion, Gloucestershire Regiment - The Glosters - 622 were either killed, wounded or taken prisoner in the fighting on Imjin River. Outnumbered and with no back up, the battalion held off an entire Chinese division of about 10,000 men after they poured across the river at midnight on April 22, 1951, in a surprise attack.*

On November 25, 180,000 Chinese troops launched a massive attack on the UN forces, driving them southward over the 38th Parallel, and capturing Seoul in early January 1951. General Walker was killed in a jeep accident, his place being taken by General Matthew Ridgway. By mid-January the Chinese attack had run out of steam and the UN forces were able to counterattack, recapture Seoul on March 14, and stabilize the front roughly along the 38th Parallel by early April.

An 03 January 1951 file photo shows US troops of the 19th Infantry Regiment working their way over the snowy mountains about 10 miles north of Seoul, Korea.

Then, on April 22, the Chinese attacked once more, but were contained by many feats of courage by UN forces, such as the epic stand of the Gloucesters at the Imjin River. A second Chinese offensive opened on May 15, but was again held and the line eventually stabilized about 20 miles north of the 38th Parallel by mid-June. The Chinese used massive numbers in their attempt to overwhelm UN forces and were eventually held by immense bombardments.

From then on until an armistice was signed on July 27, 1953, the war settled down to WWI-type trench warfare, both sides occupying trenches, blockhouses, and strongpoints on opposing hill features, with limited attacks, patrolling, and other small-scale operations taking place for the next two years. These actions were just as bitter and hard-fought as anything that had gone before, but for most of the time intermittent peace talks were taking place at Kaesong, just inside communist lines, and they dragged on for some time, especially frustrating for the men at the front. The 37 months of hostilities had cost the UN forces some 72,500 killed, 250,000 wounded, and 84,000 captured or missing (many of whom died in captivity); the Chinese and North Koreans lost a total of 1,350,000 killed and wounded.

This 09 June, 1951 image shows a young girl with her brother on her back as she walks past a stalled M-26 tank at Haengju, Korea.

This 04 Sept, 1951 photo shows four F4U's (Corsairs) returning from a combat mission over North Korea, circling the aircraft carrier USS Boxer while waiting to land.

A Young Mao Tse Tung addresses his followers.

1950–59

The Chinese occupation of Tibet—like all wars—can be seen from various angles: that of the Buddhist perspective against a communist ideology that was almost its invert; or that of the Tibetan nation opposing a Chinese state implacably restoring its hegemony. On the wane in the 20th century, China is ancient and patient, and Tibet had been a documented part of the Middle Kingdom for over 700 years. Since the 19th century the "Great Game" played by the competing European powers had began to nibble away at her borders, demanding concessions and encouraging breakaway elements. However, following the end of World War II and the settling of matters between the CCP and the KMT, Mao Tse-tung consolidated his grip on the country and sought to oppose any continued western attempts to wrest Tibet from the newly proclaimed People's Republic.

Thus on October 7, 1950, Chinese forces invaded eastern Tibet and soon occupied Chamdo, sweeping aside a poorly equipped Tibetan Army, only approximately 10,000 strong and no match for a Red Army seasoned by over 20 years of continuous combat. However, the geography of the Tibetan plateau, with an average elevation of 12,000ft above sea level, caused much greater problems for the invaders, who had to negotiate two of the highest passes in the world—Shargung-la (16,700ft) and Tro-la (17,100ft). But come they did—the 15-year-old Dalai Lama having to be smuggled out of Lhasa secretly as the capital was occupied by Chinese troops on December 21, to set up temporary government at Yatung, near the border with Bhutan. Nine months later he realized the futility of armed struggle against such massive forces and, opposed to further bloodshed, was brought back to Lhasa where he was held by the Chinese. By October Tibetan independence was over, but the struggle was not.

Young monks expect the procession of the Dalai Lama, around 1950.

The same fundamental difference in approach that had put Communism and Buddhism on a confrontation course, combined with growing resentment at the strain on the country's resources imposed by the Chinese presence, led to a serious rebellion among the Golok tribesmen of Kham province in eastern Tibet in March 1956. They are reputed to have massacred an entire Chinese garrison of 8–900 men. In retaliation, the Chinese bombed Golok villages—with heavy civilian casualties. Sporadic revolts continued to occur over the next three years, funded by western financial and military support.

This simmering period finally culminated in a large-scale rebellion in March 1959, whose failure would lead to the final flight of the Dalai Lama from Tibet. The revolt started in Lhasa on March 17 and lasted for several days. By the time it had been quelled by Chinese troops, at least 2,000 Tibetans had been killed, two large monasteries totally destroyed, and thousands of monks put in concentration camps or condemned to forced labor. The Dalai Lama fled from Lhasa on March 17 with a retinue of 80 and reached the Indian frontier on March 30. Nehru braved Chinese wrath to offer him sanctuary. He lives on the Indo-Tibetan border to this day—and a miniature Buddhist Tibet has grown up around him.

List of participants:... China, Tibet
Duration:................. 1950–59
Location:................. Tibet
Outcome:................. China occupies Tibet
Casualty figures: 65,000

Vo Nguyen Giap, commander of the Vietminh Observes Dien Bien Phu Batt siege.

1946–54

In the mid-19th century, the increasingly technological European societies continued to exploit and colonize the rest of the world. So the ancient country of Vietnam became a colony of France, along with Tonking, Annam, Laos, Cambodia, and Cochin-China, all of which, between 1863 and 1892, had become French protectorates and were known collectively as French Indo-China. By the 1930s a nationalist movement had begun, and by 1941 had been forged into a political party, the Vietminh, by Ho Chi Minh, a fervent Vietnamese communist and nationalist educated in Paris and Moscow.

The Vietminh, cooperating with and supported by the Allies, fought against the Japanese, who occupied the country throughout World War II. In 1945, after the collapse of Japan and before the western powers had time to return, the Vietminh declared Vietnam an independent nation and set up a nationalist government under Ho Chi Minh in Hanoi.

However, France, with British and American collusion, reestablished control by March 1950, driving the Vietminh out of Hanoi as far north as the 16th Parallel. The French controlled the towns, but not the countryside, and beyond the 16th Parallel Ho Chi Minh's regime, commanded in the field by Vo Nguyen Giap, was well established under the protection of the Nationalist Chinese.

Commander Vo Nguyen Giap and his officers plan their attack on the French.

The French continued to build-up troop numbers in an attempt to contain the Vietminh; they also received financial and military support from the U.S. in 1950–54. However, it was to no avail—their supply lines and bases were thousands of miles away, while the Vietminh had a well-organized and much shorter supply route, as well as the sympathy of most of the population. The Vietminh were also ideologically and patriotically inspired to enormous sacrifice, fighting in human waves careless of their own survival to overwhelm the French, despite their firepower and the enormous casualties taken to achieve victory. Under this relentless pressure the French forces could not cope. Finally, late in 1953, Vietminh forces engaged the French in the last major battle of the war in the far northwest corner of the country, at Dien Bien Phu, an isolated and almost indefensible site. The French were surrounded, and the battle turned into a prolonged and horrible siege, with the French position steadily deteriorating and having to be supplied by air until it was overwhelmed. On May 7 the French surrendered; 11,000 men were taken prisoner. With this last battle the defeated French left the country.

List of participants:... Vietminh, France
Duration:................. 1946–54
Location:.................. Vietnam
Outcome:.................. French defeated and expelled
Casualty figures:....... 600,000

The French Prime Minister Charles De Gaulle in Algeria.

1954–62

France conquered and colonized Algeria in 1848, after prolonged indigenous resistance. Resurgent Algerian Islamic nationalism became active in the early 1920s and resumed at the end of World War II, the most dominant group being the Front de la Libération Nationale (FLN). On VE-Day, May 8, 1945, Muslim extremists killed 103 Europeans; in retaliation the Army killed 500 Muslims and the colonists (Colons or Pieds Noirs) murdered a further 6,000. The colonists were then gradually forced to withdraw into the cities as the FLN began to take over the countryside.

The revolution is generally regarded as having actually started on November 1, 1954. In the early morning hours the FLN launched attacks in various parts of the country against military installations, police outposts, warehouses, communications facilities, and public utilities—at the same time issuing a general call to arms.

In retaliation colonist vigilante units assassinated suspected FLN members of the Muslim community, at the same time demanding the proclamation of a state of emergency, the banning of all groups advocating separation from France, and the imposition of capital punishment for politically motivated crimes. So far the majority of the population had not risen against the Government; however, to escalate the situation the FLN deliberately targeted civilians and executed 123 people at Phillipeville, including women and children. This made the government take on as its policy the colonists' demands for repressive measures against the rebels. Government forces claimed to have killed over 1,000 guerrillas in retaliation for Phillipeville. The war correspondingly spread nationwide.

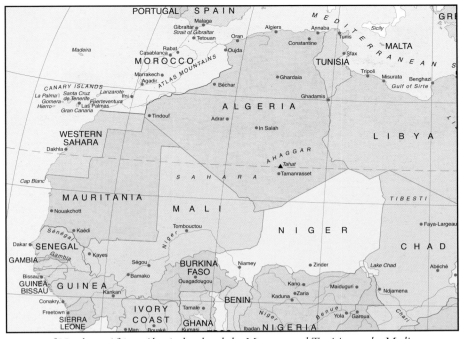

A Map of Northern Africa, Algeria bordered by Morocco and Tunisia on the Mediterranean.

By 1956 France had more than 400,000 troops in Algeria. During 1956 and 1957, the FLN continued their classic guerrilla warfare, specializing in ambushes and night raids while avoiding direct contact with superior French forces. In response, the French Army sealed the borders to limit infiltration from Tunisia and Morocco, and divided the country into sectors that had permanent troops responsible for local security. At the same time, they applied collective responsibility to villages suspected of supplying the guerrillas, and even resettled some of the rural population into camps under military supervision. This began to constrain the FLN.

Both Muslims and Europeans felt new hope for an end to the conflict when Charles de Gaulle was returned to power in 1958. In 1958-59, the French Army switched tactics to that of mobile forces deployed on massive search-and-destroy missions against known FLN strongholds. In September 1959, de Gaulle changed his stance on Algeria and spoke of self-determination. Claiming that de Gaulle had betrayed them, the colonists, with the backing of elements of the French Army, staged insurrections in January 1960 and April 1961, but these were minority events that could not prevent the inevitable. Talks with the FLN began in Evian May 1961, with a cease-fire agreed on March 19, 1962. On July 1, 1962, some 6 million of a total Algerian electorate of 6.5 million cast their ballots in the referendum on independence. The vote was nearly unanimous. De Gaulle pronounced Algeria an independent country on July 3.

List of participants:... FLN, France
Duration:................ 1954–62
Location:................ Algeria
Outcome:................ Algerian independence
Casualty figures: 500,000

The terrorist leaders of the Greek Cypriots, who destroyed the Republic of Cyprus in the name of Enosis. Archbishop Makarios, General Grivas and the present Greek Cypriot leader Glafcos Clerides welcoming the Greek army to Cyprus in 1964.

1955-60

As a Mediterranean island, Cyprus has changed hands often. It was under Ottoman Turkish rule for over 300 years from 1570 until 1878, when the island's administration was taken over by the emerging new power, Britain. Formally annexed to the British Crown in 1914 when Turkey joined the German side in World War I, in 1915 Britain offered to cede Cyprus to Greece in return for their entry into the war against Germany. Greece, expecting a German victory, declined.

When Britain's annexation was recognized at the Treaty of Lausanne in 1923, the island then became a Crown Colony. This was the trigger to begin a campaign for Enosis (Union) with mainland Greece, for the majority of the population, being Greek, looked to Greece as their home country. The Greek Orthodox Church led and fostered the Enosis movement and in 1931 the first serious riots on the island had to be suppressed by the British authorities. In 1950 a Michel Mouskos was elected as Archbishop Makarios III. In 1951 Makarios then recruited Georgios Grivas, a retired Greek Army colonel and Cypriot, to form the National Organization of Cypriot Fighters (EOKA) as the military wing of Enosis. With the beginning of EOKA's campaign, ethnic tensions rose considerably between the Greeks and Turks, manifest itself in increased sectarian violence. Villages were besieged, vendettas pursued, ambuscades and assassinations carried out.

Now a crucial influence on the future of events took place, with the moving of Britain's HQ Middle East Command, from Egypt to Cyprus in 1954. This made Cyprus into a vital strategic base for British forces and was followed by a British statement that Cyprus would never be granted independence and the UN's refusal to consider the Cyprus question.

Lt Col The Marquis of Douro, CO of the Royal Horse Guards, salutes Surgeon Captain G C Wilson, shot dead in his car by Eoka on his way to treat a Greek Cypriot civilian on 7 August 1958.

EOKA waged a terrorist campaign that targeted primarily the British and also continued to terrify the Turkish population, and a propaganda campaign that sought to gain the full acceptance of the Greek population and influence world opinion. By deporting Makarios and increasing the number of troops to 40,000, the British were eventually able to restrain Greek Cypriot unrest, but they could not win over the hearts and minds of the people.

In March 1959 Makarios returned to Cyprus as part of a deal to forgo Enosis and replace it with a Cypriot republic. A furious Grivas returned to Greece. In December Makarios was elected as the first President of Cyprus, with the Turkish Cypriot Rauf Denktash as his deputy, and EOKA was forced to declare a cease-fire. On August 16, 1960, Cyprus was granted independence as a republic within the British Commonwealth. This political settlement did not last long as in 1974 EOKA staged a coup d'etat, declaring Enosis with Greece, at that time itself controlled through similar methods under the regime of the Colonels. Turkey, alarmed at such events so close to her coast and in order to protect the interests of the Turkish minority, launched a massive invasion of northern Cyprus. Partition then ensued, with a line of demarcation being supervised by UN peacekeeping forces. However, the problem has not been solved nor gone away; the divisions remain to this day, as do the British military bases. Cyprus is a thorn in the side of Turkey's attempts to join the European Union.

List of participants:... EOKA, Britain, Turkey
Duration:................. 1955-60
Location:.................. Cyprus
Outcome:.................. Independence for Cyprus without union with mainland
　　　　　　　　　　　　 Greece. Turkish invasion
Casualty figures: 500

British paratroopers, alert and with their weapons ready, sit on a captured Russian-built, Egyptian Army tank at Port Said. Egypt announced that fierce fighting had broken out again in Port Said and had continued into the next day.

OCTOBER 31–NOVEMBER 7, 1956

In some ways the Suez Crisis was another manifestation of the Cold War, for its roots lay in the decision by the U.S. and Britain not to finance the construction of the Aswan Dam as they had originally intended. This change of heart came about as a result of the growing link between Egypt and the Soviet Union, itself a consequence of American and British support for Israel. A militant President Nasser reacted to the refusal by declaring martial law in the Canal Zone and seizing control of the Anglo-French Suez Canal Company, boasting that as a national asset it would soon pay for the dam's construction. Britain and France were angry at the commercial loss and motivated to act by the fear that Nasser might close the Canal completely and cut off oil supplies from the Persian Gulf to the west. Their interests also coincided with Israel's—for Nasser, fully rearmed by the USSR, was on the point of another attempt to destroy the new Jewish state.

When diplomatic efforts failed to settle the crisis, Britain and France decided that the only way to ensure free passage through the Suez Canal was to capture it by force of arms. This plan was made in conjunction with Israel, the ruse being that she would invade first, and Britain and France would then "step in" to prevent further fighting and keep the canal open. So, on October 29, 1956, Israeli forces invaded Egypt in a preemptive strike. The next day Britain and France, following the plan, demanded that Israeli and Egyptian troops withdraw from the Canal, and announced that they would intervene to enforce the cease-fire immediately ordered by the UN.

The only Suez airfield in Allied hands is at El Gamel, where British airborne troops made a landing during the first assault.

Nasser rejected this ultimatum, and on October 31, Operation "Musketeer" was launched—the capture of the Suez Canal by British and French forces, beginning with sea and air operations. The first ground force involvement was the dropping of more than 1,000 British and French paratroops near Port Said on November 5. On the 6th there were seaborne assaults by British and French Commandos on Port Said and Port Fuad, with tank support. All objectives are taken and the operation was militarily successful. But it did not succeed. Intense U.S. and UN pressure then forced Britain and France to agree to a cease-fire on November 7, having advanced only some 30 miles down the canal. The U.S. had been caught by surprise by this dual invasion, its Cold War concerns more focused on the unrest in Hungary than with Britain and France's problems with Egypt.

The last Anglo-French forces left by the end of December, having been replaced by a UN Emergency Force (UNEF). Nasser emerged from the Suez Crisis a hero for the cause of Arab nationalism. Israel did not win freedom to use the Canal but it did regain its shipping rights in the Straits of Tiran, as well as considerably more territory.

List of participants:... Britain, France, Egypt, Israel
Duration:................ October 31–November 7, 1956
Location:................. Egypt
Outcome:................. British and French succumb to international pressure and leave
Casualty figures:....... 10,000

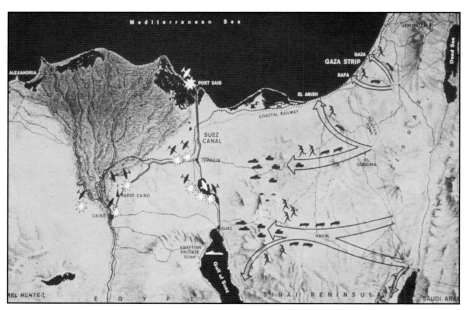

A Map of the Suez canal and vicinity.

OCTOBER 29–NOVEMBER 7, 1956

The Suez Crisis and war of 1956 were a combination of colliding ideological and religious tectonic plates that included the Arab-Israeli schism, the global Cold War rift and the final fling of European ex-colonial powers in that region.

With the rise of President Nasser in 1954 Egypt became the driving force behind Arab nationalist ambitions, and frequent raids were mounted from the Egyptian controlled Gaza Strip, used by Arab guerrillas for raids into southern Israel.

On May 22, 1956, Egypt closed the Straits of Tiran to all Israeli shipping and all ships bound for Eilat. This blockade cut off Israel's essential supply route with Asia and the flow of oil from its main supplier, Iran. In June the last British troops, whose presence restrained Egypt from attacking Israel, left the Canal Zone and Egypt started to prepare for war. In July Nasser nationalized the Suez Canal and in September Israel, France and Britain concurring in their fears of being cut off from critical supply routes, began planning a joint military campaign against Egypt, with the understanding that Israel would take the initiative by seizing the Sinai Peninsula. The British and French would then "step in" and occupy the Canal Zone in order to separate the two sides.

On October 29 the order was given to attack Egypt and Israel launched Operation "Kadesh." In less than a week its forces had reached the eastern bank of the Suez Canal, seizing the Gaza Strip and nearly all the Sinai Peninsula and storming the West Bank and then the Golan Heights.

The Suez canal is a major trade route and provides the locals with much of their economy.

The Sinai operations were then supplemented by an Anglo-French invasion of Egypt on November 5, giving the allies control of the northern sector of the Suez Canal.

The war was brought to a halt by a UN General Assembly resolution calling for an immediate cease-fire and withdrawal of all invading forces from Egyptian territory. A United Nations Emergency Force (UNEF) was then created to replace the British and French troops and by December 22 they had left Egypt. However, Israel delayed her withdrawal, until it had received a guarantee against further Egyptian attack. After several additional UN resolutions and pressure from the United States, Israeli forces finally left in March 1957.

List of participants:... Israel, Egypt, Britain, France
Duration:............... October 29–November 7, 1956
Location:.............. Middle East
Outcome:............... Stalemate
Casualty figures: 10,000

The Red Star is prominent over this square - flanked by Parliament and the Communist Party headquarters - scene of heavy fighting in Budapest, the capital, during the so-called Hungarian October Revolution.

OCTOBER 23–NOVEMBER 14, 1956

Since the end of World War II Hungary, along with the rest of Eastern Europe, had been treated by Russia according to Stalin's policy of subservient client buffer states: controlled with an iron rod by Moscow. In a climate of fear and paranoia, the hard-won freedoms of the people were stolen away by their supposed guardians. Finally, with the death of Stalin in 1953, there was a hiatus and a temporary relaxing of the reins.

In July 1953 the hated Soviet puppet Rikosi was replaced by Imre Nagy, who at once instituted a more liberal regime. This brief glimpse of what might be sowed fresh seeds of Hungarian nationalism. However, by April 1955 Moscow resumed control, expelled Nagy from the party, and reinstated Rakosi along with his old hard-line policies. This return to the hated old ways, combined with a bad harvest, bad weather, and fuel shortages brought unrest from a simmer to the boil.

By 1956 the situation had become critical. In July the new Russian leader, Khrushchev, made the a token gesture of removing Rakosi, but refused to reinstate Nagy: the uprising was only a few months away. It was destined to be very brief—from beginning to end the revolution lasted only 18 days.

On October 23, 1956, students and workers took to the streets of the capital Budapest, influenced by Poland, who had won concessions from the Kremlin earlier in the year by street protests and displays of rebellion. Hungary decided to follow suit.

By popular demand Imre Nagy was reinstated and appointed Prime Minister, with Janos Kadar as foreign minister. These appointments were initially accepted by Moscow in an attempt to defuse the situation; as a

A Statue of Imre Nagy hero of the Hungarian revolution.

further gesture, the Red Army even pulled out, restricting themselves to borders and bases. Nagy then set about encouraging all political parties to reform and had the famous Cardinal Mindszenty—fearless critic of the Russians—released from prison.

Then it all went too far for the USSR. On October 31, in a radio broadcast, Nagy announced that Hungary would withdraw itself from the Warsaw Pact and asked the UN to recognize the country as a neutral state. Kadar immediately resigned from the government and established a rival one in eastern Hungary protected by Soviet armor. More tanks then stormed Budapest and set about restoring order with immense brutality—machine-gunning protesters and crushing them with their tracks. Nagy was tried, executed, and buried in an unmarked grave. By November 14, "order" had been restored. Kadar was put in charge, and Soviet rule had been reestablished. The popular but powerless rebellion had been doomed, but the cynicism of its suppression dealt a severe blow to Communism in general and Stalinism in particular. Such repression also sent a chilling message to workers across Eastern Europe, and drove the political revolution underground. To flee these reprisals, some 200,000 people left for the west. At the time, and with hindsight, many thought that the west should have intervened. Given the geographic location of Hungary, any help attempted from the west could well have triggered Armageddon, and any economic boycott of the Soviet Union would have been pointless as Russia took what it needed from the countries it occupied.

List of participants:... USSR, Hungarian public
Duration:................. October 23–November 14, 1956
Location:.................. Hungary
Outcome:................. Uprising savagely repressed by the Soviets
Casualty figures: 23,000

L'Imam Ahmad at the end of 1950.

1963–67

The British won Aden from the Sultan of Lahej in 1839, and developed it as a coal depot for ships passing through to India and the Dominions. Aden consisted of the port and a town that grew up around it in the crater of an extinct volcano which creates the natural harbor. The stretch of mainland was known as the hinterland and was divided into two areas—the Eastern and the Western Protectorates. These were populated by Muslim Arabs who were almost continuously at war with each other, but whose rulers were content to enter into treaties with Britain. With the rise in Arab nationalism and the loss of their military bases in Egypt, Britain's smaller territories became strategically more important to safeguard the flow of oil from the Persian Gulf, and so it was with Cyprus and Aden. Britain's aim then was to foster the development of Aden and her Protectorates into a friendly self-governing state.

For the most part the sheikhs and sultans of the upcountry tribes, fearing domination by the Adeni townsmen and communism, chose to continue their association with Britain. The trade union movement in the town of Aden, however, wanted to slough off the colonial yoke altogether. By 1959 ten states in the Western Protectorate had signed treaties with Britain and formed the Federation of Amirates of the South. On January 18, 1963, when Aden also joined, it was then renamed the Federation of South Arabia, with Britain promising independence no later than 1968 but reserving the right to maintain a military base in perpetuity. With the clock ticking down to independence, three rival factions lined up to do battle: the Organization for the Liberation of the Occupied South (OLOS), the National Liberation Front (NLF)—both backed by Egypt—and the Saudi-linked South Arabian League (SAL), with the British in the middle vainly trying to keep the peace.

Captain Roger Bannister of the Royal Army Medical Corps, waves as he boards a plane at Blackbushe Airport on his way to take up an Army posting in Aden.

Against these elements Britain fought a difficult campaign supported haphazardly by local forces—the Federal Regular Army (FRA) and the Federal National Guard (FNG). They also had continual trouble from upcountry tribesmen, especially in the Radfan hills, where Operations "Nutcracker" in January 1964 and "Radforce" in May 1964 were designed to restrict rebel operations. In January 1966, OLOS and the NLF combined to form the Front for the Liberation of Occupied Yemen (FLOSY). The more conservative SAL, resenting the influence of Egypt, broke away. In February 1966 the British Government then announced that no military presence would be maintained in Aden after independence, and with that all hopes of a peaceful solution vanished. In November FLOSY split into its component parts and started fighting each other. From this internecine battle the NLF emerged victorious and by 1967 had also gained control of the South Arabian principalities. Britain withdrew in November 1967, transferring power to the NLF which then formed the single-party government of the new People's Republic of South Yemen—the name being changed to the People's Democratic Republic of the Yemen (PDRY) on November 30, 1970.

List of participants:... Britain, FRA, FNG, OLOS, NLF, SAL
Duration:................ 1963–67
Location:................. Aden
Outcome:................. NLF win the race for domination before independence
Casualty figures: 2000

Two young Tamil Tiger guerrillas show off their machine gun 12 August in the eastern town of Vakarai where they established training facilities after being driven out of northern town of Jaffna earlier this year.

1971–TO DATE

The island of Sri Lanka, located off the southeast coast of India, is home to two ethnic groups, the Sinhalese and the Tamils. The British took control of Ceylon, as it was then known, in the early 1800s, and when they left in 1948, they installed a form of government that essentially gave the Sinhalese control of the entire island. Although in a majority with 80 percent of the population, the enduring Sinhalese prejudice against the Tamils triggered a fierce liberation movement, that drew on support from Tamil Nadu—the nearest Indian province—with 60 million sympathetic Tamils that can sustain their cousins on the island.

When the British left, the United National Party (UNP)—a multi-ethnic coalition drawn from the island's English-educated elite—assumed power, but among the Sinhalese majority, nationalism grew and soon a new party emerged—the Sri Lanka Freedom Party (SLFP) led by Bandaranaike. 1971 was the turning point and the beginning of the civil war that engulfs Sri Lanka even today. The SLFP won the 1971 elections and the following year Ceylon was renamed the Republic of Sri Lanka, with a new constitution making Buddhism the state religion and Sinhalese the official language. That same year the first radical Tamil separatist movement emerged—the Liberation Tigers of Tamil Eelam (LTTE), also known as the Tamil Tigers, lead by Velupillai Prabhakaran. LTTE demanded an independent Tamil state (Eelam) in the northern and eastern provinces of Sri Lanka. By 1983 clashes between the national army and LTTE had escalated into civil war and the government declared a state of emergency in response to Tamil Tiger attacks on army installations, politicians, and Sinhalese civilians. During the next two decades, the Tamil Tigers become well known for their ferocity—including "Black Tiger" suicide missions of bombers

Eighty-six people were killed when suspected members of the Liberation Tigers of Tamil Eelam detonated an explosives-laden truck that ripped apart office buildings in central Colombo, the Sri Lankan capital.

who killed themselves along with their targets. In July after the killing of some Sinhalese soldiers, hundreds of Tamils were killed in riots across the capital city Colombo, and most of the Tamil-owned businesses were systematically targeted and destroyed. More than 100,000 Tamils then fled to India, bringing the Indian government into the situation. On July 29, 1987, the India-Sri Lanka Accord was signed, giving the Tamils an autonomous province in northeast Sri Lanka and providing an Indian Peacekeeping Force (IPKF) to police this region. LTTE opposed the accord vehemently and began to target both the Sri Lankan army and the IPKF. After three years of thankless and costly attempts to prevent the crisis from escalating, the IPKF gave up and left, leaving LTTE in control of much of northern Sri Lanka. In May 1993 LTTE struck again when a suicide bomber killed the Sinhalese President Premadasa during a May Day parade. The newly elected president, Chandrika Kumaratunga, called a truce and restarted the peace talks with the LTTE in January 1995, and the rebels appeared to compromise when they stated that they would accept some kind of federal system, rather than complete independence. However, by April negotiations had broken down again and LTTE resumed their campaign of violence. In October the Sri Lankan government launched a massive new offensive against LTTE which two months later in December took the Tamil stronghold of Jaffna. None of the underlying issues have been resolved and the Sri Lankan civil war continues. In 2004 the Asian Tsunami devasted the entire country, it may yet bring an end to their troubles.

List of participants:... Sinhalese government, LTTE, IPKF
Duration:............... 1971–
Location:................ Sri Lanka
Outcome:................ Ongoing
Casualty figures: 50,000

Ho Chi Minh at the founding of the Republic of Vietnam.

1954–65

It is difficult to be precise about the date of American involvement in Vietnam, for the United States entered into war gradually between 1950 and 1965, as the Cold War became more defined and positions hardened. Certainly the U.S. always regarded the enemy there to be the Vietminh and the communist government of North Vietnam, both led by Ho Chi Minh. To the Americans, communism was a contagious disease that would spread unless prevented: it had to be fought at all costs. In the late 1940s the French and British, allies of the U.S., were loath to give up their colonial possessions in Asia, which had valuable resources that could help restart their economies ravaged by World War II. Thus in May 1950, President Truman, pursuing his doctrine of military and economic aid to any nation threatened by communism, authorized financial and military aid to the French, who were fighting to regain control of their Indochina colony, including Laos and Cambodia as well as Vietnam. In spite of this assistance, the French were not successful and following their defeat at Dien Bien Phu in 1954 and the consequent formation of North Vietnam, north of the 17th Parallel, the south of the country was thrown into complete turmoil. This is when the U.S. first began to go in on the ground, in an attempt to build up a bulwark against further communist expansion. First, a government was formed from religious leaders and Army generals; second, a few U.S. military advisers were sent to train a South Vietnamese army; third, the Central Intelligence Agency (CIA) was activated to conduct psychological and propaganda warfare against the north.

The 1954 Geneva Peace Agreements had provided for a Demilitarized Zone at the 17th Parallel and a national—combined North and South— election to be held to determine "the national will of the Vietnamese people." The election did not take place: instead in October 1954,

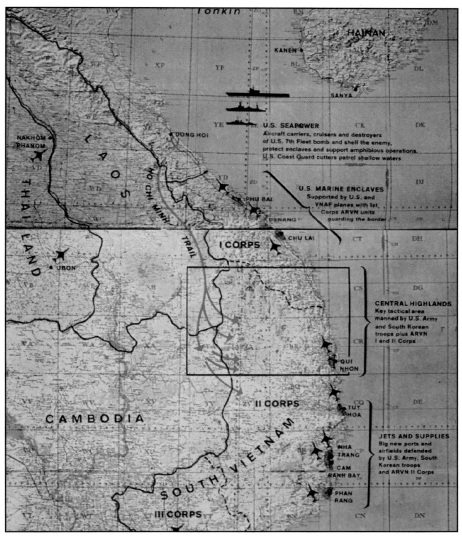

Battle of Ap Bac Jan. 2, 1963 in Mekong Delta.

President Eisenhower publicly committed the U.S. to supplying direct aid to the South Vietnamese government. Ratified by the U.S. Senate in 1955 and signed by the President, the Southeast Asia Treaty Organization (SEATO) treaty promised aid to any nation to contain communism. The flow of military advisers began to increase. The next president to become involved was Kennedy, who passed another and perhaps even more important milestone in early 1961, when he secretly sent 400 Special Forces to teach the South Vietnamese and the Montagnard tribes opposed to the communists how to fight guerilla jungle warfare. By the time Kennedy was assassinated in November 1963, there were more than 16,000 U.S. military advisers in South Vietnam. more than 100 had already been killed.

List of participants:...U.S., North and South Vietnam
Duration:................. 1954–65
Location:................. Vietnam
Outcome:................. Escalating war
Casualty figures: 150,000

A combo of the Indonesian Sukarno political sibling rivals (L- R) father and founding president Sukarno, current Indonesian President Megawati Sukarnoputri, heading the Indonesian Democratic Party of Struggle (PDIP), Rachmawati Sukarnoputri heading the

1962–65

Sarawak, Brunei, and Borneo were all close to independence in 1962, for Britain had formulated a plan to incorporate these territories into a Malaysian federation, along the lines of similar accommodations it had made to other colonies at that time. However, President Sukarno of neighboring Indonesia had an agenda of his own. A militaristic, tough nationalist, trying to balance the two great power blocs in his nation—the Communist Party of Indonesia (PKI) and the Army—he hoped that his opposition to the British would keep both of them on his side. Seizing the opportunity to increase the size of Kalimantan, the Indonesian name for their part of the island of Borneo, he began his campaign of Konfrontasi—confrontation. To begin with, on December 8, 1962, pro-Indonesian rebels in Brunei tried to capture the sultan who appealed to the British for help. They replied promptly by airlifting in two companies of Gurkhas from Singapore. Over the next few days other units were also flown in and the rebellion was quickly suppressed. Undeterred, Sukarno escalated the situation by authorizing cross-border incursions in order to intimidate the local population and destabilize the situation. Britain responded by importing another five battalions of British and Gurkha troops under the command of Major-General Walker, who was faced with the almost impossible task of policing a mountainous jungle border 1,000 miles long. Walker, however, was the ideal man for the job—a veteran of both Britain's World War II battle against the Japanese in the jungles of Burma, and also the more recent counter-insurgency operations in Malaya. His approach was carefully considered and consisted of three different strands: first, the meticulous gathering of intelligence; second, the initiation of a proactive jungle-patrolling regime to dominate that environment as much as possible; third, winning the hearts and minds of the local population by establishing medical and agricultural projects to improve their

Pioneer Party (PP) and Sukmawati Sukarnoputri, the head of Indonesian National Party (PNI). The three daughters of Sukarno, who headed Indonesia's independence struggle and was president between 1945-1966 before being toppled by the military, have continued the political dynasty and will all lead their parties in the general elections.

living conditions. Local tribesmen friendly to the government were then recruited into an irregular force named the Border Scouts. These measures soon resulted in the successful containment of Indonesian attempts at destabilization.

In September 1963 Sukarno took another fateful step and ordered regular Indonesian troops over the border in small groups of 200 or so, to establish bases in the jungle and beef up the guerrillas. The British responded by increasing their troops to 13 battalions of infantry— including all eight battalions of the excellent jungle fighters the Gurkhas, plus a battalion of SAS, along with artillery and engineer support. Troops were also provided by Malaysia, Australia, and New Zealand.

With these resources at his disposal, Walker then answered like with like by moving his bases nearer the border, supplied and reinforced by helicopter. He became still more preemptive by taking the battle over the border in spoiling raids of his own. By the time he handed over command, his approach had succeeded and by late 1965 the Indonesians had lost control of the frontier and the situation. In March 1966 President Sukarno was removed in a coup by the anti-communist General Suharto. Malaysia and Indonesia then signed a peace treaty in August and the Confrontation was over.

List of participants:	Britain, Indonesia
Duration:	1962–65
Location:	Borneo
Outcome:	Indonesia repulsed
Casualty figures:	13,500

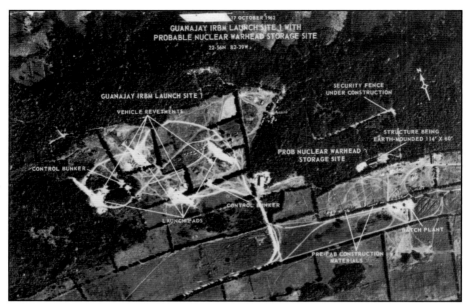

October 17, 1962: U-2 photograph of first IRBM site found under construction.

OCTOBER 15–28, 1962

The event that has become known as the Cuban Missile Crisis was the closest the world has ever come to nuclear war—so far. It was certainly the hottest point of the Cold War, with the United States' armed forces at their highest state of readiness to attack, and Soviet field commanders in Cuba prepared to use their newly installed nuclear weapons to defend the island if it were invaded. The roots of this particular crisis lie in the nuclear arms race between the two superpowers. In 1962 the USSR was lagging behind the U.S., with Soviet missiles only powerful enough to be launched against Europe, while American missiles were capable of striking anywhere in the USSR. Trying to alleviate this imbalance swiftly, Soviet Premier Nikita Khrushchev conceived the idea of deploying Soviet intermediate-range missiles in Cuba, thereby doubling the Soviet strategic arsenal and providing an effective deterrent against any potential American attack on the Soviet Union. President Fidel Castro was also looking for a way to defend Cuba from another attack by the U.S. ever since the failed Bay of Pigs invasion in 1961. He consequently backed Khrushchev's plan and in the summer of 1962 the Soviet Union set about secretly building its missile installations in America's backyard, on the island of Cuba.

The crisis really began on October 15, 1962, when the U.S. first became aware the sites were under construction through covert reconnaissance photography. When President Kennedy was informed, he immediately gathered a dozen of his closest advisors around him and went into closed session. Several days of intense debate later, they decided to impose a naval blockade around Cuba, to prevent the arrival of any more Soviet missiles, and to go public with the situation. October 22, Kennedy detailed what had occurred in Cuba and his response. He also announced that any nuclear missile launched from Cuba would be

November 6, 1962: Soviet personnel and six missile transporters loading onto ship transport at Casilda port. (Note shadow at lower right of RF-101 reconnaissance jet taking the photograph.)

regarded as an attack on the U.S. by the USSR and would be responded to accordingly. He finished by demanding that the Soviets remove all of their offensive weapons from Cuba immediately.

Tensions began to build on both sides. Kennedy eventually ordered low-level reconnaissance missions once every two hours and then pulled the naval blockade back and raised military readiness to DEFCON 2. On the 26th Kennedy received the first of two letters from Khrushchev. In it he proposed removing the Soviet nuclear missiles and personnel, if the U.S. would guarantee never to invade Cuba. The following day was the worst day of the crisis—a U-2 spy plane was shot down over Cuba, and Kennedy also received the second letter from Khrushchev proposing another exchange—the removal of U.S. missiles in Turkey in return for the removal of the Soviet missiles on Cuba. This caused a major quandary until the Attorney General Robert Kennedy suggested agreeing to the first letter and ignoring the second. The Soviet Ambassador in the U.S. was then contacted and informed of the U.S. agreement to the conditions of the first letter, without any mention at all of the second.

On October 28 Khrushchev responded positively, expressing his confidence that the United States would not invade Cuba and announcing that the Soviet missiles would be brought back to the Soviet Union and with that the crisis had passed.

List of participants:... U.S., USSR, Cuba
Duration:................. October 15–28, 1962
Location: .... Cuba
Outcome:................. USSR dismantles its Cuban-based nuclear missiles
Casualty figures: .... Spy plane shot down

President Lyndon B. Johnson delivers "Midnight Address" on 2nd Gulf of Tonkin incident in Vietnam.

JULY 30–AUGUST 7 1964

With the benefit of hindsight, the Tonkin Incident was the event that the U.S. used to involve itself further in Vietnam. As we have seen, the South Vietnamese government was completely reliant on this American support and U.S. military advisors had arrived to further assist with counter-insurgency operations and train a South Vietnamese Army. Naval operations were also expanded, with reconnaissance missions carried out off the coast of North Vietnam and it was here, in the Gulf of Tonkin, that the incident took place.

The United States only acknowledged a three-mile national territorial limit to North Vietnamese waters and not the 12-mile limit claimed by the North Vietnamese. On the nights of July 30 and 31, 1964, two North Vietnamese islands—Hon Me and Hon Ngu—were shelled, the exact source of the attack a mystery. On July 31 the U.S. destroyer Maddox entered the area and by August 2 was not far from Hon Me when three North Vietnamese torpedo boats came speeding toward her from the island. Having fired warning shots to no response, the Maddox opened fire on the approaching boats, who also began firing and launching their torpedoes. Two of the North Vietnamese boats were damaged in the exchange and returned to shore with the other one covering their flight; one shell hit the Maddox.

The U.S. responded by sending a stern warning to the North Vietnamese that unprovoked attacks would not be tolerated. However, the American area of operations continued to remain within the 12-mile zone claimed by the North Vietnamese. On August 4, 1964, two U.S. destroyers—the Maddox, again, and the C. Turner Joy—were again on patrol in the Gulf of Tonkin when radar images indicated that they were being approached by speeding vessels. Both ships then fired repeatedly into the night.

President Lyndon B. Johnson signs "Gulf of Tonkin" resolution (Joint Resolution for the Maintenance of Peace and Security in Southeast Asia).

On hearing of this second incident President Johnson went to Congress to get approval for a proposed air strike, which was granted and carried out the next day. The President announced the action on television as a retaliatory raid for the second unprovoked attack on U.S. ships—which the North Vietnamese denied.

On August 7, Congress passed the Tonkin Gulf Resolution giving the president the authority to use any measure necessary to deal with aggression in Vietnam. With it the U.S. effectively committed itself to a war that would cause it much grief in the future.

List of participants:... North Vietnam, U.S.
Duration:................. July 30–August 7 1964
Location:.................. Gulf of Tonkin
Outcome:................. Escalation to war
Casualty figures: 30

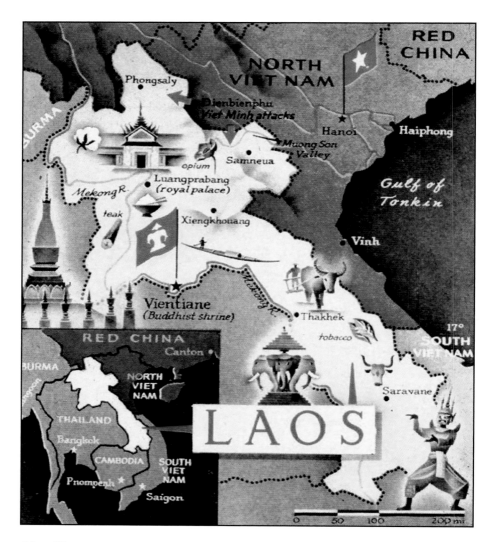

Map of Laos

Off Vietnam, the heavy cruiser USS Canberra (CAG 2) became the first US Navy vessel to relay operational message via communication satellite, using the Syncom III to reach the Naval Communications Station in Honolulu, 4,000 miles away.

South Vietnamese soldiers walk along a trail in Laos, where they operated in unfamiliar territory, against strong enemy forces long: entrenched there in violation of Laotian sovereignty and the 1962 Geneva Accords on Laos.

First U-2 group to Vietnam, got there on 5 March 1964.

Santo Domingo, Dominican Republic-Dominican Preisdent Juan Bosch (l) and U.S. Vice-President Lyndon Johnson.

1961–66

From the 1930s to the 1950s, the Dominican Republic was ruled by the dictator Rafael Leónidas Trujillo Molina, known in the United States simply as Trujillo. This despot treated the country as his own personal fiefdom, enforcing his power with murderers and cronies, and keeping the public in subjection through violence and manipulation—by conjuring a xenophobic hatred of Haiti, the other country who shared the island. After his long-deserved assassination by young army officers in 1961, there was a state of flux, in which members of the military and Trujillo's sons jockeyed for power. The U.S. then intervened, mindful of the island's proximity to Cuba and determined to prevent another country in what it considered to be its own backyard falling to communism. President Kennedy insisted that free elections be held and the Trujillo family promptly fled abroad to live off its Swiss bank accounts. The people then threw themselves wholeheartedly into elections, enjoying political freedom for the first time. Many new political parties began, with only the Communist Party outlawed in deference to the United States.

The new President was Juan Bosch of the Dominican Revolutionary Party (PRD). An academic and writer, he had spent years in exile as an activist opposed to the Trujillo regime and was an anti-communist reformer. So Bosch and the PRD Government began a program of land redistribution and a general strengthening of the labor movement, at the same time reorganizing the army and applying the separation of church and state as detailed in the new constitution. In doing so they ran up against the conservative forces in Dominican society, who began to feel increasingly threatened. Landowners, businessmen, Catholic religious leaders, and high-ranking army officers all began to complain bitterly at the loss of their opportunities, powers, and privileges while resenting

US Marines drive down a street in Santo Domingo during the occupation of the Dominican Republic in 1965.

the reforms and the new freedom of speech. Accusing Bosch of bringing communism in by the back door, they believed that he was about to turn their country into another Cuba. Such a fear soon reached the ear of the American ambassador and alarm bells began to sound in the U.S.

Bosch would not compromise with these conservative forces, and was consequently toppled in a bloodless coup carried out by the military on September 3, 1963. Having forced him to flee into exile again, a puppet civilian government was installed in an attempt to disguise the fact that the military was in control. For the next two years the Dominican Republic reeled in economic and political chaos, with things getting progressively worse. Finally in April 1965, a group of officers rebeled against their own regime and led an attempt to restore Bosch to power. The fighting soon spread to civilians and after a few days the rebels seemed to be getting the upper hand. The same conservative elements as before saw the bogey of a communist insurrection and turned again to the U.S. President Johnson, feeling threatened by events in Vietnam and wanting to be seen as an aggressive fighter of communism, decided on a show of strength. Under the guise of an Inter-American Peace Force and with the backing of Latin members of the Organization of American States, he sent in 42,000 Marines. Bosch was then prevented from returning to power and in 1966 a new more pro-American president was elected.

List of participants:... U.S., PRD, Dominican Army
Duration:................. 1961–66
Location:................. Dominican Republic
Outcome:................. Pro-American president elected
Casualty figures: 3,000

A group of tribesmen prepare to fight during the war between India and Pakistan.

APRIL–SEPTEMBER 1965

Following partition India and Pakistan remained in a state of uneasy peace, with conflict ready to occur at any time anywhere along their long shared frontier. On April 9, 1965, just such an event occurred in the Rann of Kutch—a desolate salt marsh through which the western end of the border ran. Sporadic fighting continued until the end of June when the Indian and Pakistani governments signed a cease-fire agreement arbitrated by the British. However, by then the war had escalated and moved north to Kashmir—another area bitterly disputed by Hindus and Moslems, through which the border also ran.

Following India's unwillingness to fight China over their border dispute in 1962, the Pakistanis had come to an incorrect conclusion that a swift campaign in the disputed territory of Kashmir, coupled with the fact that the majority of the population there were Muslim, would certainly meet with success. The ensuing operation was codenamed "Gibraltar." On August 5 Pakistani irregulars slipped over the border and invaded east Kashmir. Incensed, India responded by rushing forces of its own into the area over the next few days and launched a counterattack on August 15—the official start of hostilities. Pakistan, since it had not used its regular army, claimed the attack as unprovoked. Initially, the Indian Army met with considerable success in the north, but this was balanced by Pakistani gains a little further south at Chamb when they,

An Indian gun control position in the Burki area during the war between India and Pakistan. The village of Burki was captured a few days after the Hodiara village.

too, brought their regular armored formations into the fray. However, India by and large had the upper hand with its numerically superior forces and reached as far as the Haji Pir Pass, five miles inside Pakistani territory. Pakistan then reactivated the western front in a move that took the Indians by surprise. They responded by launching a three-pronged offensive aimed at Lahore, Operation "Grand Slam," spreading conflict into two new areas with attacks near Sialkot and north of Gadra toward Hyderabad. Air power was brought to bear by both sides in order to check their opponent's attacking forces. Far from being an easy victory for either side, the war reached stalemate. On September 20 the UN Security Council demanded a cease-fire, and a few days later the fighting died down. There were no great gains—each side held bits of the other's territory along what was a disputed border and none of the underlying reasons for the conflict were resolved.

List of participants:... India, Pakistan
Duration:.............. April–September 1965
Location:................ India and Pakistan
Outcome:................ Stalemate
Casualty figures: 20,000

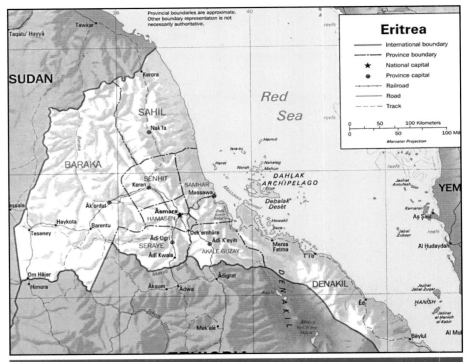

1958–93

After World War II Haile Selassie had been brought back from London and reinstalled as emperor. Not wishing to be dragged into any Eritrean-Ethiopian arguments, Britain then simply referred the whole matter to the UN. The UN awarded Eritrea to Ethiopia in 1952 as part of a federation of the two states, which pleased the Ethiopians because it gave their landlocked country access to two major Red Sea ports at Massawa and Assab. The Eritreans, on the other hand, were devastated—for Ethiopia has always sought to incorporate Eritrea into its territory. Disappointment and protest then simmered before breaking out in demonstrations and marches in 1958. The Ethiopian response was to suppress the disturbances militarily, with troops killing many protestors in the process. By the early 1970s there were two major opposition groups: the Eritrean Liberation Front (ELF) and the Eritrean People's Liberation Forces (EPLF). Both defined themselves as Marxist parties in opposition to the Ethiopian monarchy and its western supporters such as the U.S.—from whom it received aid in return for its service as a key listening post in the Middle East. Emperor Haile Selassie was losing his hold on the government and in 1974 was deposed and killed by a military junta—the "Dergue." The Dergue also called themselves Marxists and so this change of regime saw the USSR replace the U.S. as Ethiopia's main supporter. Soon the Ethiopian Army was equipped with large amounts of Soviet weaponry. In 1977 the Dergue leader, Mengistu, seized absolute power in a coup that caused a civil war to break out within Ethiopia itself and left many thousands of people dead. While Mengistu consolidated his hold on power the Ethiopian Army suffered a series of defeats against the fast-moving hit-and-run tactics of the ELF and EPLF, who had successfully liberated various Eritrean towns, Mengistu reorganized the military in preparation for a massive counterattack. By the time the rebels tried to retake the Eritrean

UN Marines in Eritrea.

port city of Massawa, Mengistu had built up his forces sufficiently to repulse and then pulverize them with a sustained barrage of artillery and airstrikes. The war then entered a new phase; Ethiopia conducted six huge coordinated offensives, that succeeded in virtually wiping out the ELF and clearing eastern Eritrea of all rebel presence. The cost, though, was appalling; for although the Ethiopians had the military equipment and advisers of a modern technological nation state, her armies up till then had been of a older, more feudal nature and their offensives were often characterized by costly human wave assaults. One by one the Eritrean towns fell again to the Ethiopians and the remaining EPLF were forced to retreat into their Sahel mountain stronghold. Then, in 1988 the tide of war turned once again, with a critical victory for the Eritreans at Af Abet, the main Ethiopian Army supply depot in Eritrea where they captured vast stores of ammunition, heavy weapons, and equipment. This timely free resupply was as valuable to the Eritrean war effort as it was demoralizing to the Ethiopians, who had reached the end of their resources—expended on a futile war rather than used to cope with crippling drought. Both were catastrophic. In May 1991, the EPLF took Decamare, the last major town before the Eritrean capital of Asmara. As the Ethiopian Army began to desert, the northern province of Tigray broke away under an anti-Mengistu liberation group, the TPLF, which then allied with the EPLF and began moving toward the Ethiopian capital Addis Ababa. Mengitsu fled into exile. In 1993 Eritrea was formally recognized as a sovereign nation and set about rebuilding itself.

List of participants:... Eritrean ELF and EPLF, Ethiopia
Duration:................. 1958–93
Location:.................. Eritrea—Ethiopia
Outcome:.................. Eritrean independence
Casualty figures: 300,000

These children of the Congo have lost their parents to civil war.

1960–65

From 1908 until independence on June 30, 1960, the mineral rich Congo was savagely administered as a Belgian colony. Its first African leaders, Prime Minister Patrice Lumumba and President Joseph Kasavubu, had barely entered office when the army mutinied, removing any authority the civilian government possessed and creating panic among the 100,000 Belgians still living in the country, mainly near the capital Leopoldville. In response to these events the Belgian government sent troops to protect its citizens. Next Katanga was declared independent by local leader Moise Tshombe, backed by various European companies and mercenaries waiting in the wings to profit from mining enterprises. Katanga is essentially the prize at the heart of all the struggles of the Congo directly as a result of its immense underground wealth. In the chaos Lumumba appealed to the UN for help: a peacekeeping force of nearly 10,000 troops was sent. It was given the task of restoring law and order, preventing other nations' involvement and helping with the rebuilding. Lumumba then demanded that this force be used militarily to depose Tshombe and reincorporate Katanga into the Congo. When this was refused, he accused the UN of colluding with Tshombe because of Katanga's rich mineral reserves. Angry at the UN failure to help, he appealed to the USSR, who provided the government with enough military equipment for an attack on Katanga. When the attempt failed Kasavubu dismissed Lumumba and appointed the Congo Army chief, Colonel Mobutu, as the new prime minister. Lumumba and his supporters promptly set up a rival government in Stanleyville in the east of the country, but he was then assassinated by mercenaries. By 1961, they were four groups disputing the country: Mobutu's government based in Leopoldville, Lumumba's supporters based in Stanleyville, Tshombe's Katangan government in Elizabethville, and another new breakaway group in the Kasai province. The three other groups then united against

UN Secretary General Dag Hammarskjold who died in a plane crash near Ndola airport on 17 September 1961 in the former Northern Rhodesia, now Zambia, where he was due to meet rebel leader Moise Tshombe to negociate a truce in the Congo civil war. Documents released by the truth commission in South Africa 19 August point to direct South African, British and US involvement in a plot to kill Hammarskjold. The documents refer to the operation under the code name "How is Celeste" and point to the involvement of the US Central Intelligence Agency and Britain's M15 intelligence agency.

Katanga and formed a new parliament in Leopoldville headed by Cyrille Adoula. When Adoula again asked the UN for military support, this time it was given: in August 1961, 5,000 United Nations troops launched an attack on Katanga, capturing key points in the province and forcing Tshombe into peace talks. But after almost a year nothing had been accomplished and in 1962 UN troops attacked Katanga again, forcing Tshombe to flee and the rebel province to be reunited with the rest of the Congo. However, by July 1964 he was back—this time elected PM of the Congo in another lightning turn-around that characterizes the virtually permanent state of flux in this bewildering area. In November white mercenaries hired by Tshombe retook Stanleyville and released 1,800 white hostages. The following year saw Mobutu's second coup, in which he ousted Tshombe finally from power. In 1996 the veteran guerrilla fighter Laurent Kabila lead an anti-Mobutu rebellion and the following year Mobutu himself finally relinquished power and fled the country, with Kabila in turn declaring himself head of state. By March 2000, a staggering 14 African countries had become involved in the stalemated conflict with the country being contested by four regional regimes, each one completely dependent upon foreign troops for its own survival. Laurent Kabila's central government controls about half the country, from the northwest equatorial region to mineral-rich Katanga in the southeast, the various rebel groups controlling the rest. All are financed by the sale of easily transported gold, diamonds, and ivory.

List of participants:... UN, Mobutu, Lumumba, (Katanga)Tshombe, Kasai
Duration:................. 1960–65
Location:.................. Congo
Outcome:................. Continued civil war
Casualty figures: 100,000

An armored tank moves toward the Parliament Building during a coup in Athens. Greek colonel Giorgio Papadopoulos took power and set up a military government during the coup.

1967–74

Though the civil war had ended in 1949, Greece had remained politically unstable, despite its entry into NATO. In the three years prior to the coup of the Colonels, the communists gained strength, formenting public unrest into demonstrations, strikes, and eventually riots. This, in turn, triggered the conservative fear of another communist attempt to seize power, although there was also an element of opportunism amongst some of the junior officers that became involved in the ensuing military takeover.

On April 21, 1967, a group of three Greek army officers—two colonels and a brigadier general—took control of the country through a classic military coup, carried out late at night and catching everyone completely by surprise without a single shot being fired. Having seized all the main lines of communication, the country awoke to be told that a state of martial law existed. The leader of the regime that came to be known as the Junta, or the Colonels, was George Papadopoulos, who assumed the role of head of state. The military then tried to rule through the king and the existing political system. However, disapproved of by the politicians who refused to cooperate with them, they soon resorted to more physical means and began to arrest all those who opposed them, at the same time consolidating as much power as possible in their own hands. In December 1967 the king attempted to organize a counter coup but with its failure he was forced into exile.

The junta's aims and policies were unclear—a mixture of paternalistic authoritarianism and populist reforms backed up by an extensive secret police network that monitored society, using torture and committing other human rights' violations. In the first three years, the main targets of this policy were known supporters of the communists, but as time went

Armored vehicle patrols street here Dec. 13 after the Greek military junta announced that King Constantine's counter coup had been crushed.

on many centrist politicians were also arrested. The regime's brutality soon made it an international pariah and Greece withdrew from the EEC in 1969, in order to avoid suspension. Nevertheless, Greece's NATO allies confined themselves to verbal condemnation because the regime fulfilled every geopolitical requirement, anchoring the alliance's defenses in the unstable eastern Mediterranean. Knowing that the Colonels were politically inexperienced, the western powers were content instead to build up the psychological pressure. In the event the dictatorship lasted for seven years and sparked an international crisis before it folded, and in that time all free elections were suspended. Eventually in their clumsy attempt to appropriate Cyprus in 1974 and its consequent aftershocks, they were forced from power.

List of participants:... The Colonels, communists, Greek public
Duration:................. 1967–74
Location:.................. Greece
Outcome:.................. Colonels toppled
Casualty figures: 1,000

Villagers watch a group of Nigerian federal troops in a Biafran town. Biafra was a region of eastern Nigeria that seceded from 1967 to 1970.

1966–70

The geographical area of Nigeria is composed of three major ethnic groups, the result of Britain's colonial administration. The eastern region—Biafra—is dominated by the Ibo, the west by the Yoruba, and the north by the Hausa/Fulani. These tribal ingredients were the usual recipe for a bitter civil war when the British left. These forcibly federated tribal areas were collectively known as Nigeria when they were given their independence by Britain in 1960. Six years later increasing ethnic tension, especially in the military, would shatter any illusion of a single entity and make the Ibo/Biafrans decided to secede from the federation and fight for their independence.

A good quality and substantial oilfield had been discovered in the southern Niger (Biafran) delta in 1958, and it quickly grew to dominate Nigeria's economy. This vital economic resource made the Hausa/Fulani and the Yoruba oppose Biafran independence. In January 1966 there was a military coup, in which Tafawa Balewa's government was overthrown by junior Ibo officers, who made a senior officer, another Ibo, head of state. Following Balewa's death massive anti-Ibo riots and attacks ensued, resulting in a massacre with over 30,000 deaths and the flight of a million Ibo from the north to the east. This made all easterners now oppose the idea of a united Nigeria, and although the Federal Military Government (FMG) made peace offerings and invited the eastern region to peace talks in Lagos, they were rejected. On May 30, 1967, Biafra formally announced itself an independent republic. In July FMG army combat units were dispatched to the east, to be met by rebel Biafran troops, who also took control of strategic points in the mid-western

Jubilant Nigerians in the streets of Lagos January 12th following ceasefire announcement and end of Biafran conflict. Federal Nigeria accepted the surrender of Biafra and pronounced amnesty for its people as Federal troops erased the 30-month-old rebel state from the map.

region. The FMG regained its control of the mid-west and delta region, and then cut off Biafran access to the sea, but by the end of 1967, they were still unable to penetrate the Ibo heartland, resulting in a stalemate. Although outnumbered and outgunned, the Biafrans had motivated leadership and high morale. The FMG then increased its forces substantially to over 250,000 men and invaded the oil-rich province of Owerri. The Biafran rebels managed to liberate Owerri, but another even bigger FMG offensive in the south finally overwhelmed them. The FMG then took a daring step, proclaiming a state of emergency in the whole country and proposing the abolition of the regions and the redivision of the country into 12 new states. This was recognized a radical attempt to change things and it succeeded in first dividing the easterners into those that accepted the concession and the hardcore Ibo who opposed it. However, without the support of all elements within Biafra opposition and independence were not viable options and in April 1968 the division of Nigeria into 12 new states was implemented, with Biafra becoming the East Central State in 1970.

List of participants: ... FMG, rebel Biafran troops
Duration: 1966–70
Location: .... Nigeria
Outcome: .... Biafra reincorporated into Nigeria
Casualty figures: .... Between one and two million

Jordanian soldiers carry a portrait of King Hussein in their jeep in this photo taken in June 1967.

JUNE 5–10, 1967

After the Suez War of 1956 the UN troops in Sinai kept the peace on the border between the Israelis and Egyptians. However, a decade later Nasser, still driven by his dream to lead a union of all Arab states, decided that Egypt was again strong enough to clash with Israel. As he began to make increasingly bombastic speeches threatening war, so the incidents between Israel and all her Arab neighbors grew more frequent and the propaganda war began to rise in tempo.

By May 1967 Egyptian forces were massing near the border, and Nasser finally ordered the UN troops to leave the Sinai and Gaza, also announcing that the Gulf of Aqaba would once again be closed to Israeli shipping, cutting off her oil supplies. At the end of that month, Egypt and Jordan signed a new defense pact and Syrian troops, too, were primed for battle along the Golan Heights.

Knowing that war was inevitable and unable to maintain a condition of constant readiness indefinitely, Israeli decided to jump before she was pushed. On June 5 she launched a series of daring preemptive air strikes on Egyptian, Syrian, Jordanian, and Iraqi airfields that by the evening of following day had destroyed the combat effectiveness of all enemy air forces. Having won air supremacy and continuing to retain the initiative, Israel next launched her armored formations into Sinai, reaching the Suez Canal and occupying most of the peninsula in less than four days. Playing a cunning holding game and dealing with her opponents piecemeal, she could use her resources to maximum effect. Jordan was next, in a lightning Israeli campaign that took Jerusalem and the West Bank by June 8. As the war then drew to a conclusion on the Jordanian and Egyptian fronts, Israel turned her attention north, to Syria.

Israeli army Major-General Ariel Sharon during the Six Day War 29 May 1967 in the Sinai desert.

In just over two days of fierce fighting with heavy casualties, Syrian forces were expelled from the Golan Heights.

The stunningly fast Six-Day War ended on June 10, when the UN negotiated a cease-fire on all fronts. By the end of the war, Israel had conquered enough territory to more than triple the size of the area it controlled and enabled her to unify Jerusalem. Through its occupation of Sinai, Gaza, Arab Jerusalem, the West Bank, and Golan Heights, Israel had shortened its land frontiers with Egypt and Jordan and removed the most heavily populated Jewish areas from direct Arab artillery range—although these occupied areas also included over 750,000 hostile Palestinians.

In November 1967, the United Nations Security Council adopted Resolution 242, which established a formula for Arab-Israeli peace—that Israel withdraw from the territories it had taken in the war in return for peace with its neighbors.

List of participants:... Israel, Egypt, Syria, Jordan
Duration:................. June 5–10, 1967
Location:.................. Middle East
Outcome:.................. Israel triples in size
Casualty figures:........ 25,000

Former Israeli Defence Minister Moshe Dayan (C) and Gen. Rechavam Zeevi (2nd, L) in conversation with the Palestinian keeper of the Cave of the Patriarchs in Hebron during the 1967 Six day war.

An unidentified destroyed armored personnel vehicle (L) is abandoned 10 June 1967 near an Israeli US-made Super-Sherman tank on the road between Jerusalem and Bethlehem, in the occupied West Bank10 June 1967. On 05 June 1967, Israel launched preemptive attacks against Egypt and Syria. In just six days, Israel occupied the Gaza Strip and the Sinai peninsula of Egypt, the Golan Heights of Syria, and the West Bank and Arab sector of East Jerusalem (both under Jordanian rule), thereby giving the conflict the name of the Six-Day War.

Czech youngsters holding Czechoslovak flag stand atop an overturned truck as other Prague residents surround Soviet tanks in downtown Prague.

AUGUST 20/21, 1968

Czechoslovakia's fortunes were the same as many other middle European countries in the 19th and 20th centuries: slow eclipse and domination, first by the Germans and then by the Russians. Before the end of World War II in May 1945, her fate had been decided by the Yalta Agreement, in which Stalin, Roosevelt, and Churchill had agreed upon the spheres of influence in a soon to be liberated Europe. So when Allied troops were only 50 miles from Prague, they stopped as agreed and allowed the Russians to enter the city—thus ensuring that Czechoslovakia would become a Soviet buffer state.

By 1948 the Party apparatus was installed and the communists were firmly in control, deciding who held what posts with little regard to popular feeling other than the token presence of Jan Masaryk, son of the first president. He was appointed foreign minister but then died mysteriously when he began to become a focus of Czechoslovakian aspirations. From then on for 20 years politically correct Party puppet dictators maintained the status quo.

As with USSR and all her satellites, the death of Stalin in 1953 had a slight relaxing effect on the control system. By early 1968, the then Russian leader, Leonid Brezhnev, was making accommodations to similar nationalist moderates in various client states that he would also later regret. This resulted in a spectrum of response according to the character and circumstances of each nation and its leader, but with nationalist resurgence the general rule. In Czechoslovakia, Alexander Dubcek was the man, impatient to ease the power of the state and the squeeze on his people. When he became First Secretary in January 1968, he immediately began to accelerate the process with a series of liberalizing reforms that by April ushered in what has become known the "Prague Spring."

Prague residents carrying Czechoslovak flag and throwing burning torches attempt to stop a Soviet tank in downtown Prague.

In spite of increasingly severe warnings from Moscow and attempts at mediation by other Warsaw Pact allies, Dubcek wouldn't compromise or be compromised any longer. With such a stance and the hardening of the Soviet response to such situations, confrontation was inevitable. On the night of August 20/21, 250,000 Soviet troops plus the obligatory symbolic contingents from neighboring Warsaw Pact countries, crossed the frontier and took over the country with a calm determination. Reacting so swiftly before the situation could develop into another Hungary helped avoid a messy end to the affair. The USSR removed Dubcek and reassumed a stricter control: Czechoslovakia then remained firmly behind the Iron Curtain until its fall in the late 1980s.

List of participants:... USSR, Czechoslovakia
Duration:................ August 20/21, 1968
Location:................. Czechoslovakia
Outcome:................ USSR reasserts control
Casualty figures: 100

File picture shows Vietcong soldiers climbing onto a US tank abandoned on a road in Hue in 1968 during the Tet general offensive.

1968

At 03:00 on the morning of January 31, 1968, the first day of Tet, the Vietnamese lunar New Year, the U.S. received a nasty shock when 70,000 North Vietnamese and Viet Cong troops launched their biggest offensive of the Vietnam war to date. Both the timing and the scale of the attack came as a total surprise, for a cease-fire had been agreed and begun only the day before on the Vietnamese new year. The attack encompassed the whole of South Vietnam, including over 100 cities, towns, military bases, and even an attempt on the U.S. Embassy in Saigon.

By the close of 1966 North Vietnam considered the war to be at a stalemate, their attempts to overrun the south checked through a combination of intense U.S. bombing of the north and stubborn fighting in the south, both of which had caused large losses of manpower and war materiel. Hanoi felt that, somehow, it had to regain the initiative and so the planning began for the Tet Offensive, headed by General Vo Nguyen Giap, the victor of Dien Bien Phu.

Ten days before the main assault, the battle of Khe Sanh took place, on the tenth anniversary of Dien Bien Phu and with a similar scenario to the original battle (with this time U.S. troops surrounded and cut off). The North Vietnamese purpose was to remind the world of that victory, to renew their own sense of mission and also as a diversionary tactic to draw American forces out of other cities.

When the Tet Offensive began, the communists consisted of the North Vietnamese Army (NVA) and the Viet Cong (VC), who were South Vietnamese civilians and North Vietnamese advisers living in cities and villages throughout South Vietnam. The NVA hoped that the action

US troops recapture the Vietnamese city of Hue after it had been taken the the Viet Cong during the Tet Offensive D.R. Howe treats the wounds of Private First Class D.A. Crum, "H" Company, 2nd Battalion, Fifth Marine Regiment, During Operation Hue City in Vietnam 06 February, 1968.

would spark off a general uprising in the south. At 03:00 that morning simultaneous attacks took place across the country, with fighting erupting in all major locations. In the north the city of Hue was completely captured by the VC, who then executed city officials and their families. In the capital Saigon, street-fighting took place and an attempt was made to storm the U.S. Embassy.

Although the shock of the attack was immense, it was actually a military disaster for the communists, for they lost over 10,000 men, did not manage to hold any of their objectives, and the bulk of the civilian population did not rebel.

However, extraordinarily, this military defeat became a political victory because of its effects in the U.S. For the war that had erupted onto the streets of South Vietnam was also beamed into American homes through the medium of television, reported in a sensationalist way by shocked journalists at source. The Vietnamese communists were much more intelligent than the U.S. gave them credit for—a classic case of underestimating your enemy. They took the time to study U.S. home news and media—the way it functioned and affected public opinion. Vietnam was the first instant media war, with many foreign and U.S. film crews operating while operations were ongoing.

List of participants:... U.S., Viet Cong, NVA
Duration:.................. 1968
Location:................... South Vietnam
Outcome:................... Offensive fails but immense propaganda advantage
Casualty figures: 50,000

Female Vietcong soldier in action with an anti-tank gun during a fighting in southern Cuu Long delta in the frame of the Tet general offensive launched in all the South Vietnam in spring 1968.

The sensationalist reporting often exaggerated and even misrepresented the facts, in the case of Tet leaving the public with the impression that the offensive had been successful, which was not the case. Tet opened up a second front—in America—through the growing antiwar movement on college campuses and in the city streets. This made the North Vietnamese cling to the belief that victory would be theirs, if they only stayed their course and America lost "because of its democracy; through dissent and protest it lost the ability to mobilize a will to win."

Saigon, South Vietnam- Houses burn during fierce fighting on the north side of this frightened capital city May 6th. Cholon, Saigon's Chinese district, was the scene May 8th of stepped up enemy terrorism, with troops scurrying from block to block firing at police stations and military vehicles and hoisting Viet Cong flags up light poles.

A mural adorning a wall of "Free Derry Corner", in the Bogside area of Londonderry, Northern Ireland.

1969–

The Normans invaded Ireland in the 12th century, and over the years later monarchs asserted British control of the island. However, it was the religious intolerance of the 16th and 17th centuries that stimulated nationalism, and over the years, the desire for freedom grew.

The first nationalist uprising of the 20th century began in 1918 in Dublin and although violently suppressed by Britain it was the start of the Irish Republican Army (IRA) and a guerrilla war that three years later in 1921 forced the British into a Partition agreement. Ireland became independent Eire with the exception of the six northernmost Protestant-dominated counties, who determined to remain within the British Union. This Protestant-Catholic divide is the key to the Troubles and remains so to this day. For in those six counties of Protestant Ulster the Catholic minority were treated very much as second-class citizens, resulting in two implacably hostile religious communities. A blatantly biased political system was designed to deny the Catholics any share in the running or the resources of the province, although their inexorable rise in population threatened in time to correct this imbalance. By the 1960s this deep fear had triggered the emergence of more extreme Loyalist groups that were vociferous in their condemnation of Catholicism. 1967 in turn, saw the formation of the Northern Ireland Civil Rights Association (CRA)—a Catholic organization campaigning to improve their political rights. In October 1968 the CRA staged a march in Londonderry leading to a riot in which 88 people were injured. Events then accelerated as the IRA resurfaced in a new virulent form, the Provisional IRA or Provos, with a campaign for a United Ireland that began in the winter of 1968–69. By the summer of 1969 the crisis in Northern Ireland had reached conflagration point, for the Protestant Unionists, who had ruled Northern Ireland as a one party state since

General Sir Robert Ford, Britain's Commander of Land Forces in Northern Ireland, pictured on July 3, 1972, in Belfast.

Partition, had no interest or experience in negotiating with the minority Catholic community for more civil rights. The Loyalist Protestant Orange Order is an organization that commemorates and celebrates the conquest of Catholicism in the 17th century. Its marching calendar has two major annual events: July 12—the 1690 Battle of the Boyne, when the Protestant King William defeated the Catholic King James, and August 12—the 1689 Siege of Derry when local apprentice boys closed the city's gates against the army of Catholic King James. This marching season never failed to inflame sectarian passions and violence between Catholics and Protestants prior to these events steadily increased. In July a Catholic civil rights demonstration in Londonderry was viciously broken up by the Royal Ulster Constabulary (RUC) and the paramilitary police known as "B Specials," so that when the marching season began things were at fever pitch. Finally the barricades went up all over the Bogside in Derry, turning it into a no-go area in order to prevent both the Orange Order from marching and the RUC from entering their community, behind which the CRA and the resurrected IRA began organizing their defense.

Sectarian clashes occurred as the Apprentice Boys marched past the perimeter of the Catholic Bogside. The RUC intervened and, assisted by a Protestant mob, charged at the nationalists forcing them into William Street. Within hours rioting had escalated. The police were stoned and petrol bombed as they made their way in riot gear into the Bogside.

List of participants:... Britain, CRA, IRA, RUC, UDA, UDF
Duration:................. 1969–
Location:................. Northern Ireland and mainland Britain
Outcome:................. Ongoing
Casualty figures: 3,325

People move to and from the Bogside area of Londonderry after a night of rioting in which at least five people were shot dead.

After two days and nights of continuous rioting, on August 14, the battle spread to Belfast and five Catholics and a Protestant were killed after the CRA called on all Catholics to take pressure off the Bogside by stretching police resources elsewhere. The following day troops were deployed in Belfast to contain the violence that had erupted from the call, but too few in number to have any effect—that night a Protestant mob burned almost every Catholic house in Bombay Street.

The British Government responded by sending in more troops to restore peace, and set about trying to make the political system fairer—against intractable opposition from the Protestants who controlled Stormont, the Northern Irish Parliament. As a result the British Government dissolved it and proceeded to govern the province directly. Though initially appreciated by Catholics as a protection against the virulent Loyalist groups and the partial police, this did not remain the state of affairs for long, for soon the IRA began shooting British soldiers and Irish policemen. The troops responded by becoming increasingly heavy-handed, turning into an army of occupation and still further alienating the Catholics.

Those suspected of being IRA were held in prison without trial. In July 1970, the Army carried out the first house-to-house search in the Falls area of Belfast and found illegal arms. On February 6, 1971, the first British soldier was killed on duty by the IRA; on March 11 the first three British soldiers off duty were killed. The escalating violence culminated on 30 Jan 1972 with Bloody Sunday, when paratroopers opened fire on a crowd of civilians in Londonderry killing 13.

The struggle then escalated still further into full-blown sectarian war, that has dragged on forty years, seeing bombing campaigns extending

Police face stone-throwing mob in the bogside area of Londonderry as an Apprentice day parade ended in violence.

to mainland Britain, assassinations, tit-for-tat murders along with compromising covert operations from the British government. The shooting for now seems to have died down with the 1997 cease-fire just holding despite the odd extremist murder. Long negotiations drag on for years with still no real end in sight. The repercussions of the anarchy of war—its denuding effects are obvious. a political culture with little real dialogue. Political organizations forced underground and funded by crime are now trapped in the cycle and committed not to their original political aims but to the criminal means. The Irish, Catholic and Protestant alike, are a hardy race who have weathered much and it is to be hoped that they will reach their own consensus—in time.

Some of the more than 8,000 human skulls, all arranged by sex and age, which rest in a Memorial Stupa at the 'Killing Fields' of Choeung Ek near Phnom Penh.

1969-75

Cambodia is an ancient Asian country peopled by the Khmer, whose lasting struggles have been mostly with neighbors Vietnam and China. In 1884, after some years as a protectorate, it was absorbed into French Indochina, ruled through a puppet monarchy. In this fashion in 1941, Prince Norodom Sihanouk came to be installed as the new king. He was, however, anything but a puppet; a fervent nationalist and communist in the mold of those times, sympathetic to the struggles against the French taking place in Vietnam and Laos. Cambodia won independence in 1953, and Sihanouk went on to dominate the Cambodian political scene for the next 15 years, By this time the Americans had replaced the French and Vietnam had become a fierce battleground, with Cambodia inevitably drawn into the conflict. Sihanouk had no choice but to allow the heavily armed and battle-experienced North Vietnamese to use Cambodia as an access corridor into South Vietnam. In February 1969, as the Cambodia-Vietnam supply route became busier, the American President Nixon sanctioned the carpet-bombing of suspected communist base camps in Cambodia. More than a half million tons of bombs were dropped by U.S. aircraft, killing thousands of civilians. The next year American and South Vietnamese troops then invaded the country in an unsuccessful attempt to eradicate the Vietnamese communist forces.

In March 1970 Sihanouk was deposed in a military coup lead by a General Lon Nol, and took refuge in China. The new government was faced with the same impossible problem as Sihanouk—how to escape further involvement in the Vietnam War. The NVA, aware of the Cambodian dissension and faced with the loss of essential supply lines, began to systematically take over the north of the country, supporting both Sihanouk's government-in-exile and the more extreme Khmer

Rouge movement, which Sihanouk himself had tried to suppress when he was in power. By 1972 the country was completely engulfed in chaos and war, with the NVA holding the east, the Khmer Rouge the north, with the U.S. bombing both and over two million refugees. The next year saw a U.S.-Vietnamese peace agreement signed in Paris. By this time a stalemate had been reached, with the NVA/Khmer Rouge controlling east of the Mekong river and also territory along the southern frontier and Lon Nol's government keeping control of most of the major towns.

The end of the stalemate came in 1975, when South Vietnam was conquered and the NVA increased supplies to the Khmer Rouge, while U.S. support ended. Phnom Penh and the government fell on April 17. Having taken the capital, the new Khmer Rouge regime, headed by Pol Pot, literally unleashed a holocaust on their own people, driving the entire population of over two million out into the countryside to set about killing or reeducating them in a systematic manner. The number of those who died between April 1975 and January 1979 has been estimated at between two and three million people—almost a half of the population.

It wasn't long before the more ancient Khmer-Viet fault opened up again, with conflict between the Khmer Rouge government of Cambodia and the communist government of a now united Vietnam. The Vietnamese invaded in 1978, easily sweeping aside the Khmer Rouge and driving them once more into the jungle. This in turn triggered the Sino-Viet rift and in late December 1978, China launched a punitive 29-day raid into northern Vietnam. The Vietnamese then set up a new government in Phnom Penh made up of Khmer Rouge defectors, but found themselves embroiled in a protracted civil war. After over a decade, they gave up trying and left.

In 1993 UN-administered elections led to a new constitution and the reinstatement of the canny survivor Norodom Sihanouk as king again. The Khmer Rouge rejected peace talks and boycotted the elections, but following a government-sponsored amnesty, defections increased so rapidly that in 1994 the Cambodian government was finally able to outlaw the Khmer Rouge. Then in July 1997 the coalition of the conservative/traditionalist National United Front (NUF) and the Cambodian People's Party (CPP) split. Elections brought the CPP to power alone despite opposition accusations of electoral malpractice. Since then Cambodia had enjoyed a period of relative stability.

List of participants:... U.S., NVA, Khmer Rouge,
Duration:................. 1969-75
Location:.................. Cambodia
Outcome:.................. NVA conquest of S Vietnam, ascendance of the Khmer Rouge
Casualty figures: 150,000

West German police negotiate with a member of the Black September terrorist group (top left) in the Munich Athletes Village where they held Israeli athletes hostage.

1971-73

In September 1971, after their defeat and ejection from Jordan, the amalgamation of Palestinian groups under the control of Yasser Arafat met in Damascus to decide on the way forward. Things were at a very low ebb—Black indeed—and something desperate was called for that could keep alive Palestinian hopes and strike back at the enemy. An escalation of extreme terrorist action against the widest possible range of targets was suggested, and although Arafat was initially fairly lukewarm about the idea, the strength of Palestinian feeling coerced him into acceptance. However, he demanded that the new terror group not be specifically associated with the PFLP/PLO and that it be given a new name to mask detection. Thus was born the Black September—made up of the most extreme members of all the leading Palestinian resistance groups.

On November 28, 1971, Black September committed its first grisly murder, when four unmasked armed men shot dead the Jordanian Prime Minister in broad daylight, then deliberately tasted his blood while chanting the Black September name. The following month they tried to assassinate Jordan's ambassador in London. These actions were supported by the majority of Palestinians, bitter with their expulsion from Jordan. The Arab states also sanctioned Black September's actions by not condemning them. With these and other raids on Israel, the Palestinian issue was kept alive and in the headlines, letting the rest of the world know that the defeat in Jordan had not destroyed the PLO or Arafat's leadership. There was no let-up, and in February 1972 members of Black September blew up a West German electrical installation and a Dutch gas plant. The group then stepped up its campaign with a series of highjackings and bomb attacks against Israel in May 1972, and it also continued to target western assets.

The remains of the helicopter that transported the Palestinian terrorists and Israeli athletes to Firstenfeldbruck NATO Airbase after being attacked by West Geman police marksmen.

The Israelis responded by assassinating members of the PFLP/PLO hierarchy, and as these tit for tat assassinations gathered pace the pressure inexorably built up,

Finally, on September 5, 1972, during the Olympic Games at Munich in West Germany, Black September pulled off another grisly coup that had the world dumbfounded. In a raid on the Olympic village they killed two Israeli athletes and took hostage another 11. In the ensuing security operation bungled by the Germans nine more athletes, five of the eight Black September gunmen, and a German policeman were killed. As the images of masked Palestinians flashed all around a watching world, Black September had gone too far—the world was appalled and disgusted and opinion turned against the Palestinians. The Israelis set about taking revenge, sending out its own hit squads, who succeeded in assassinating two out of the three Black September terrorists who survived the Munich shootout, plus a dozen others involved in the planning. This culminated in March 1973 with the assassination in Beirut of three top PLO leaders—Kamal Adwan, Mohammed Yusuf Al Najjar, and Kamal Nassar.

All this became too much for Arafat: with world opinion turned against the Palestinian cause and the decimation of his command hierarchy, he decided it was time to stop the terror campaign in the west and disband Black September.

List of participants:... Black September, Israel, the West
Duration:................. 1971-73
Location: .... Multiple locations
Outcome:................. Dissolution of Black September, but continuation of
                            problem
Casualty figures: 200-300

Idi Amin, the former president of Uganda. Amin, who seized power in 1971 and was ousted in 1979 after a bloody reign of terror.

JANUARY 1969

Uganda became a British Protectorate in 1894 following the usual route of European colonialism and was granted independence in 1962. The country is mainly divided between two major peoples: the Nilotic in the north and the Bantu in the south, with the normal chaotic group of tribal kingdoms arbitrarily lumped together by an alien administration, the largest of which was Buganda in the south. The British had recruited their security force mainly from the north, which had resulted in a northern military dominance.

Dr. Milton Obote, a northern Lango, succeeded in creating a coalition in the 1950s that led to the country's independence on the condition that Buganda would be an autonomous region. Kabaka, the king of Baganda, became the new nation's president, with Milton Obote the Prime Minister. However it became clear that Obote was an autocrat, unwilling to share power and thus making confrontation inevitable. Moving fast, he arrested many of his own cabinet ministers and ordered his army chief of staff, Major General Idi Amin, to attack the Kabaka's palace. Amin, another Muslim Lango, had risen up through the ranks to command the respect of the troops. Ruthless, popular, an ex-heavyweight boxing champion of Uganda, his rise was meteoric when Obote selected him to become the instrument of his policy. Amin accomplished his tasks: Kabaka was exiled and the Bagandan monarchy abolished. Obote, rewriting the constitution to consolidate almost all powers in the presidency, then promptly declared himself president and nationalized all foreign assets. Obote now felt threatened by Amin's popularity within the army and so began to engineer his downfall by initiating various conspiracies. Foolishly, he left Uganda to attend a Commonwealth conference in Singapore while events in Uganda spiraled out of control. His plan to have Amin arrested over missing funds went awry and the

A picture taken 26 June 1972 shows (from L) Syrian President Hafez al-Assad, President of Uganda Idi Amin Dada, Egyptian President Anwar El Sadat and Lybian leader Muammar Kadhafi in Kampala during an OUA summit.

tables were turned when Amin seized control of the military, killing Obote's conspirators. The January 1969 coup was so swift Obote did not return home but went straight into exile in Tanzania. All political activities were quickly suspended and the army was ordered to shoot anyone who was suspected of opposing the new regime. It was the beginning of a decade of complete mayhem. Seldom has a whole country been prey to whims of one insane man. For Idi Amin Dada was a full blown psychopath who went on to make international headlines and account for 300,000 of his own countrymen's heads.

In 1979, Amin was finally toppled by Ugandan rebels and Tanzanian troops, and fled the country to spend his last years in exile as a devout Muslim in Saudi Arabia. The following year Obote was reelected president and established a multi-party democracy. But the army remained unwilling to submit to his control and in 1985 he was deposed in a second military coup. Yoweri Museveni has been president of Uganda since 1986.

List of participants:... Followers of Milton Obote, Idi Amin
Duration:................January 1969
Location:.................Uganda
Outcome:.................Ascendancy of Amin
Casualty figures:........300

A crowd cheers a truckload of guerrillas after the revolution which made East Pakistan into Bangladesh succeeded. 1971.

MARCH–DECEMBER 1971

When the British finally left India in 1947 Hindu-Muslim ethnic tensions soon made some kind of partition inevitable and The following year Hindu India and Muslim Pakistan emerged from the violence. Unfortunately though Pakistan was not one continuous geographical area, the provinces of Sind, Punjab, Baluchistan and the North West Frontier being situated to the west of India, and the other half of the country—the Pakistani part of Bengal—1,000 miles away to the east. The West spoke predominantly Urdu and the East exclusively Bengali, while both halves had populations of similar sizes. However the political and therefore economic emphasis was centered almost exclusively in the western half of the country. This imbalance was the key to the Pakistani civil war. As Bengali awareness of the situation grew, so too did a political party to fight for change—the republican Awami League. In 1958 with the support from West Pakistani republicans the League won a majority in the elections and came to power, but were immediately forced out of office by a military coup under General Ayub Khan. Having arrested the Awami party leader Sheikh Mujib, Khan then remained in power for a decade. Finally in 1969, he was succeeded by General Yahya Khan who pledged to restore democracy with elections scheduled for December 1970. Again they were won overwhelmingly by the Awami League, taking 167 of 300 seats in Pakistan's National Assembly. The largest party in the western half of the country was Zulfikar Ali Bhutto's Pakistan People's Party (PPP).

The Awami League's majority encouraged them to demand independence for East Pakistan but the West rejected this—opposed to any secession, Yahya and Bhutto were both determined to keep Pakistan as a single state and on March 1, 1971, Yahya suspended the National Assembly. The League responded by calling a general strike in the East

At the Dacca Race Course, Gen. Jagjit Singh Aurora (left), Chief of Staff of the Indian Army, and Lt. Gen. Assan Ali Khan Niazi of the Pakistani Army sign the papers that would end the war between the two countries and lead to the creation of Bangladesh.

which was followed by a complete breakdown in negotiations. The West then launched an attack on East Pakistan to force it back into union, while the leaders of the League fled to India and declared East Pakistan independent as the People's Republic of Bangladesh. A brutal war ensued, Bengali resistance to the invasion taking the form of guerrilla warfare, with logistical support from India. When millions of Bengali refugees then crossed over the border into India to avoid the violence, the Indians felt sufficiently involved to justify a full scale invasion of East Pakistan in December 1971. Their massive army easily outnumbered and expelled the West Pakistani troops, and the Awami League became the government of an independent Bangladesh in January 1972. Post-independence Bangladesh's history has been beset with problems, for the country is prone to frequent natural disasters and is one of the world's poorest and most over-populated. The military has never relinquished power.

List of participants:... India, Pakistan, Bangladesh
Duration:................. March–December 1971
Location:................. Pakistan, Bangladesh, India
Outcome:................. Bangaledeshi independence
Casualty figures: 300,000

Warship HMS Fearless where British Prime Minister Harold Wilson, Ian Smith, the leader of rebel Rhodesia met off Gibraltar in October 1968, attackers sabotaged an aircraft from the flight used to transport Harold Wilson to the talks.

1960–80

Rhodesia took its name from empire builder Cecil Rhodes and its arbitrary administrative borders forced three different tribes together: the Ndebele, the Shona, and the "tribe" of white Rhodesians fighting to maintain their colonial advantages. These three groups consisted of: the Ndebele Zimbabwe African People's Union (ZAPU), with its military wing the Zimbabwe People's Revolutionary Army (ZIPRA), founded by Joshua Nkomo in 1961 and backed by the USSR; the Shona Zimbabwe African National Union (ZANU), with its military wing Zimbabwe National Liberation Army (ZANLA), founded by Ndabaningi Sithole and Robert Mugabe in August 1963 and backed by China; and the white Rhodesian Front (RF), with its military wing the Rhodesian Security Forces (RSF). Both ZAPU and ZANU professed to be Marxist-socialist African nationalist liberation movements—the rhetoric unsuccessfully hiding what they were: tribal groups. Until the question of majority rule had been decided, the African Ndebe-Shona rift was put on hold and the ZAPU-ZANU alliance concentrated on the white Rhodesians. The British government also supported majority African rule and so on November 11, 1965, the white minority Rhodesian Front (RF) government, led by Ian Smith, made a unilateral declaration of independence (UDI) and though condemned internationally set about defending its advantages.

A long messy guerrilla war then followed, gradually spreading across the whole country, with the RF slowly forced onto the defensive. Finally, the time came for compromise and a solution was concocted whereby elections were held in April 1979 with the few smaller moderate nationalist African parties who had not taken up armed struggle allowed to take part. The United African National Council (UANC), headed by Methodist Bishop Muzorewa, won a majority, but his government was

Guerrilla leaders Joshua Nkomo (L) and Robert Mugabe (R) signing the Rhodesia ceasefire agreement for the Patriotic Front at Lancaster House in London.

refused international recognition because the two largest African parties, ZAPU and ZANU, had been proscribed. The war was then renewed with increasing ferocity. In 1980, with international approval, the British stepped in again to force a settlement and an end to hostilities. The first all-party multi-racial elections were held, despite the intimidation and violence carried out by both sides. Unsurprisingly, Robert Mugabe's majority Shona ZANU party won. On April 18, 1980, the country became independent as the Republic of Zimbabwe, and its capital, Salisbury, was later renamed Harare.

Mugabe then set about subjugating firstly ZAPU and Nkomo, then any opposition within his own ZANU party, while at the same time rewarding cronies and treating the country as his own personal resource. Violence and intimidation became rife, the judiciary was compromised and corrupted, the press and opposition systematically intimidated and imprisoned, and the population manipulated against the white minority. An increasingly bizarre Mugabe rules the country to this day, originally as Prime Minister, and from 1988 as President.

List of participants:... RSF, RF, ZAPU-ZIPRA, ZANU-ZANLA
Duration:................. 1960–80
Location:................. Zimbabwe (then Rhodesia)
Outcome:................. White minority government toppled
Casualty figures:....... 12,000

Moundou, South Chad: Kindergateners learn about nutrition at a morning milk break in Moundou.

1965–72

Chad was a French protectorate from 1900, a part of French Equatorial Africa from 1908, an autonomous republic within the French commonwealth from 1959, and then a fully independent republic on August 11, 1960. This cleared the way for the real rift to manifest itselfo—a racial and religious difference between the Arab north and the south. By the mid-1960s two guerrilla movements had emerged, both northern, opposed to the existing government (based in the south), and fighting for reduced French influence and closer ties with other North African Muslim Arab states. These were the Front for the National Liberation of Chad (FROLINAT), established in 1966 and operating in the north from southern Libya, and the smaller Chad National Front (FAN) operating out of the east central region of the country.

In August 1968, President Frangois Tombalbaye asked for French military support for government troops besieged by rebels from the northern regions, but France gave air support only. However, in March 1969, the government again had to call for French assistance and French troops then became directly engaged in the maintenance of civil order. By the end of 1969 there were about 2,500 French troops in the country. The French encouraged reform and with the stability of their troops the country was calm throughout 1970–71. Tombalbaye compromised, made reforms, freed political prisoners, and included more Muslim northerners in the government. French intervention was officially ended on September 1, 1972.

However, after this Tombalbaye's government began to unravel—his southern and military power base were eroded by his compromises with the Muslim north. On April 13, 1975, several units under the initial direction of junior military officers, killed Tombalbaye during a mutiny.

Northern Toubou rebels train in Chad's Tibesti Mountains. In the mid 1960s, northern Muslim tribes began to grow angry at the southern-contolled government, with their discontent eventually leading to a full civil war between the north and south.

The emergence of the Supreme Military Council (Conseil Supérieur Militaire—CSM) began a war with FROLINAT and FAN both supported primarily by Libya. This struggle has continued for over 20 years, with the advantage constantly changing sides. Despite movement toward democratic reform, power remains in the hands of a northern ethnic oligarchy and Chad is being further destabilized by other wars in the region.

List of participants:... FROLINAT, FAN, Government forces, France
Duration:................ 1965–72
Location:................. Chad
Outcome:................. Ongoing civil war
Casualty figures: 3,050

Chile's former president Salvador Allende (R) with his then-army commander Gen. Augusto Pinochet (L) during a ceremony in Santiago. Pinochet overthrew Allende and ruled Chile with an iron fist until 1990 before returning to Chile's army command.

11 SEPT 1973-90

Chile achieved independence with the victory over the Spanish at the Battle of the Maipo River on April 5, 1818, and thereafter built up a fairly successful democracy with a legislature and independent judiciary, elected local and regional bodies, free trade unions and media, and broad-based civil liberties. However, with the growth of popular Marxism in South America, nationalism set itself against the established private ownership and American companies in order to improve the lot of the poorest elements of society. In the 1970 elections Dr. Salvador Allende became the first ever democratically elected Marxist head of state. While his administration was democratic and generally respected civil rights, it began an economic restructuring of Chile along Marxist lines. American-owned copper companies and large estates were seized. Allende then ordered a price freeze and authorized increases in wages as an income-redistribution measure. He also heavily inflated the currency to cover deficit spending, and within two years the economy was in shambles—his regime had led to increasing social and economic chaos. Had there been time, no doubt elections could have been held and Allende replaced democratically but it was not to be. By then fear of communism had forced the U.S. to actively support and encourage the Chilean military to remove its own government. The United States government undoubtedly played a key role in Allende's fall and Pinochet's subsequent rise to power.

On September 11, 1973, Chile experienced its first coup when army and air force units attacked the presidential palace. It was reported afterward that Allende had committed suicide. Augusto Pinochet became president and Chile was turned overnight from one political extreme to the other—a tottering socialist democracy to a rightist authoritarian state. Though Pinochet's repressive regime did much to restore the health

Gen. Augusto Pinochet (C) posing with unidentified army officers in Santiago, Chile, a few days following the 11 September bloody coup he led to overthrow leftist president Salvador Allende.

of the country's economy, Chile's traditional democratic freedoms had vanished. A reign of terror followed the coup in which tens of thousands of Chileans underwent torture, hundreds of thousands were forced or fled into exile, and the democratic institutions of the country were systematically destroyed. The coup leader, General Augusto Pinochet, remained military dictator of Chile for 17 years until 1990. He later also became the first dictator to be tried by an international court when, old and ill, he was arrested in Europe having come across the Atlantic for medical treatment.

List of participants:... U.S., Chilean Army, Chilean elected government
Duration:................ 11 Sept 1973-90
Location:.................. Chile
Outcome:................. Death of Allende, rise of Pinochet
Casualty figures:....... 20,000

Israeli soldiers atop a US-made Super-Sherman tank on Syria's Golan Heights, a week after the beginning of the Yom Kippur War. 06 October 1973.

October 6–24, 1973

The Yom Kippur War was the next instalment in a seemingly never-ending process of internecine strife that will not stop until the Palestinians and Jews reach a lasting accord. The Six-Day War had not settled anything: the Arabs refuseed to recognize Israel's new boundaries until a solution was found that also acknowledged the rights of the Palestinians and the Israelis refused to give up what were now buffer areas between the active Arab frontline states until it received acknowledgement of its right to exist and respect for its borders.

Israel even constructed a chain of defensive positions along the east bank of the Suez Canal, known as the Bar-Lev Line, and dug in on the Golan Heights. The Arabs retaliated with commando raids and artillery bombardments. This period was known as the War of Attrition.

In September 1970 President Nasser died and was succeeded by Anwar Sadat who took over the preparations for war and the threatening of Israel with a similar line in bombastic speeches. He was also simultaneously conducting a diplomatic offensive among European and African states to win support for the cause. Nothing concrete seemed to be happening; the Egyptian premier doing what had been done many times before. But on October 6, 1973, at Yom Kippur, the holiest day in the Jewish calendar, Egypt and Syria opened a coordinated surprise attack against Israel.

An Israeli British-made Centurion tank moving forward to the Syrian front lines on the Syrian Golan Heights, is overtaken 17 October 1973 by a United Nations (UN) jeep.

At least nine Arab states, including four non-Middle Eastern nations, actively aided the Egyptian-Syrian war effort—Iraq, Saudi Arabia, Kuwait, Libya, Algeria, Sudan, Morocco, Lebanon, and Jordan.

Thrown onto the defensive during the first two days of fighting, Israel mobilized its reserves, eventually repulsed the invaders, and carried the war deep into Syria and Egypt. The Arab states were swiftly resupplied by sea and air from the Soviet Union, which rejected U.S. efforts to work toward an immediate cease-fire. As a result, the United States belatedly began its own airlift to Israel. Two weeks later, on October 24, Egypt was saved from a disastrous defeat by the UN Security Council's timely cease-fire. The Arabs had been mauled and repulsed again, but despite ultimate success on the battlefield, Israel considered the war a diplomatic and military failure.

List of participants:... Israel, Egypt, Syria, Iraq, Saudi Arabia, Kuwait, Libya, Algeria, Sudan, Morocco, Lebanon, and Jordan
Duration:................. October 6–24, 1973
Location:.................. Middle East
Outcome:.................. Arabs repulsed again
Casualty figures: 25,000

A destroyed Soviet-made Syrian 57mm anti-aircraft gun and ZIL truck 17 October 1973 are abandoned on the Syrian lines on the Golan Heights.

An Egyptian prisoner-of-war sitting in front of victorious Israeli soldiers flashing V-signs after they establised a salient on the West Bank of the Suez canal.

Kyrenia, Cyprus:Turkish troops dig in at a gun position.

JULY–SEPTEMBER 1974

When the Colonels' regime in Greece was stumbling to its inevitable end, as with many military regimes it looked for a suitably ambiguous national cause celebre to turn attention away from their own inadequacy. Thus Cyprus was selected and the ghost of Enosis resurrected by reactivating EOKA. By April 1974 concrete evidence had been amassed by Cypriot intelligence to indicate that an EOKA coup was being planned, supplied and funded by the military government in Athens. By July 1974, Makarios narrowly escaped death in an attack by the Greek-led National Guard and fled to London, though still acknowledged by the UN as the legitimate president of the Republic of Cyprus. Meanwhile, the EOKA terrorist Nicos Sampson was declared provisional president of the new government. This rang alarms bells in Ankara and Turkish armed forces were put on alert while the Turkish prime minister Bülent Ecevit flew to London in an attempt to elicit British aid to solve the problem, as called for in the 1959 Treaty of Guarantee. The British didn't respond, choosing to sit on the fence—as did the United States.

The Turks issued a final demand for the removal of Nicos Sampson and the Greek officers from the National Guard and a guarantee of Cypriot independence. When this was not forthcoming, the Turkish invasion fleet put to sea. The final moments for any kind of peaceful solution ticked away and the Greek bluff was called. The invasion began early on July 20, 1974, and caused the collapse of the junta in Athens.

Turkish troops made an amphibious landing on the northern coast of the island around Kyrenia with a simultaneous assault by about 1,000 paratroopers on the capital Nicosia.

Turkish soldiers stand on a tank outside Farmagusta ten days after they launched their invasion of Cyprus.

By the time a cease-fire was agreed three days later, they held some 30 percent of the island and many Greek Cypriots had fled their homes.

Two unproductive conferences in Geneva followed, the first between Britain, Greece, and Turkey and the second with the additional attendance of Greek Cypriot and Turkish Cypriot representatives. Throughout this time Turkish troops steadily consolidated their occupation. On August 14, in spite of the fact that talks were still being held in Geneva and just as agreement seemed about to be reached, the Turkish army mounted a second full-scale offensive, occupying Famagusta and the Morphou area. The advance halted on a line which was the original one proposed by Turkey as the demarcation of partition in 1965. This line has come to be known as the Attila line.

The UN was still deployed on the island when Turkey invaded in 1974, and they remain there to this day, as do several thousand Turkish troops. Now, 30 years later, the island is quiet. The Greek half is in the European Union, while the Turkish half—which only Turkey recognizes as an independent state—was shrewdly kept out by a Greek Cypriot referendum on reunification voted on last April. Thirty years later, the Cyprus "problem" is still unresolved.

List of participants:... Turkey, Greece, Cyprus
Duration:................ July–September 1974
Location:................. Cyprus
Outcome:................. Partition of Cyprus
Casualty figures: 5,000

An Angolan boy cleans the boots of a Cuban soldier in Luanda. Cuban troops helped the regime of Angola's Marxist President Agostinho Neto in the recent Civil War.

1975–2002

The Portuguese were the first Europeans to arrive in Africa and the last to leave. They colonized Angola in the late 15th century; in 1951 it became a Portuguese overseas territory.

In 1961, an independence movement was formed, and the Popular Movement for the Liberation of Angola (MPLA), launched its first attacks against the Portuguese colonizers. Two other ethnically based nationalist movements were also started a little later in the mid-1960s, the National Union for the Total Independence of Angola (UNITA) and the National Front for the Liberation of Angola (FNLA).

A revolution in Portugal in 1974 brought a left-wing military junta to power; immediately, negotiations were opened to prepare Angola for independence, which was proclaimed in November 1975. The new Portuguese government, together with the three rebel movements, reached an agreement on Angola's independence. However, all three movements were determined to achieve political supremacy: the MPLA with support from the Soviet Union and Cuba, and the two other movements with the backing of South Africa's apartheid regime and the United States. The MPLA controlled the capital, Luanda, declared a people's republic, and introduced Marxism-Leninism as the official government ideology. The ensuing civil war caused an exodus of 350,000 Portuguese settlers and the collapse of thousands of Portuguese-owned farms and small businesses. This mass evacuation left Angola with very few skilled people.

The FNLA and UNITA would not recognize the new MPLA government under President Aghosineto, who eventually extended their control to most of the country, especially the major cities and the

The destruction to civilian property during this 27 year war left millions homeless.

important enclave of Cabinda with its oil industry. UNITA, however, controlled most of the rich diamond-producing areas, which enabled Savimbi to finance an almost limitless struggle. With arms largely supplied by the Cold War superpowers, the war dragged on throughout the 1980s. It was only with the final collapse of the Soviet Union and growing pressure for the dismantling of South Africa's apartheid system that the way was paved for the first serious peace negotiations between the MPLA and UNITA. In May 1991, the two sides signed the Bicesse Accords that detailed a cease-fire and elections. The ruling MPLA party won the ensuing 1992 elections, but UNITA refused to accept the results and the civil war resumed with new ferocity—over 300,000 people are believed to have been killed between 1992 and 1994 alone. In 1993, the UN Security Council imposed sanctions on UNITA. The Angolan government, after increasing its oil revenues and purchasing more military hardware, was able to retake the military initiative. In 1994, the two sides signed a new peace initiative, the Lusaka Protocol—again never fully implemented because of UNITA's unwillingness to genuinely negotiate. After four years' frustration in 1998, the government launched another full-scale offensive against them. With further UN sanctions and growing dissent within UNITA itself, the balance of power began to tip in favor of the government. What finally made the difference was the death of UNITA's Jonas Savimbi in February 2002. Six weeks later, on April 4, the two sides signed a cease-fire, offering Angola the first real prospect of peace since independence.

List of participants:... MPLA, FNLA, UNITA
Duration:................. 1975–2002
Location:.................. Angola
Outcome:.................. Eventual peace
Casualty figures: 1,500,000

File photo dated 20 October 1981 near Guelta Zemmur shows the son of late French President Francois Mitterrand, Jean-Christophe, while he was journalist at AFP, visiting the Moroccan army following an attack by the Polisario Front.

1976–91

The Spanish Sahara is mostly desert, but is also one the world's largest sources of phosphates—and just off its coast are very rich fishing grounds. It was first made a colony by Spain in 1884, though its precise borders were disputed with France. In the first few decades after World War II, with the rise in nationalist movements, the Spanish were giving their colonies independence and so the scene was set for a struggle and the players emerged—Morocco, Mauritania, and Algeria all desired to incorporate the Spanish Sahara into their own nations. The groups on the ground were the radical Algerian-supported Popular Front for the Liberation of Saguia el Hamra and Rio de Oro (POLISARIO Front), the Moroccan-backed Liberation and Unity Front (FLU), and finally the Spanish choice, the Sahrawi National United Party (PUNS), a more moderate indigenous organization. Initially the POLISARIO Front emerged as the most dominant and active of these liberation groups, beginning a guerrilla campaign in late 1974. In May 1975 after a fact-finding mission, the UN declared that no neighboring state had any historic claim over the territory and recommended a referendum of the people of the Spanish Sahara to determine their own future. This never took place. The Moroccans reached an agreement with Mauritania, then pursued their own claim, with the king leading a three-day peaceful invasion by 350,000 civilians across the border into Spanish Sahara. This tipped the balance and the Spanish ceded authority to joint Moroccan-Mauritanian control in February 1976. However, as the Spanish left, the POLISARIO Front proclaimed the Saharan Arab Democratic Republic and a little later Algeria backed its ally by breaking off diplomatic relations with Morocco and Mauritania. With the sides drawn, the civil war then escalated, the POLISARIO Front taking the battle to the enemy by attacking the Mauritanian capital Nouakchott. By this method within two years they succeeded in breaking up the Moroccan-Mauritanian

The Polisario front, an armed movement backed by Algeria, is fighting for the independence of Western Sahara, a former colony of Spain that was invaded and annexed by Morocco in 1975.

alliance, culminating in the Mauritanian president being deposed in a bloodless coup. In August 1979, a peace treaty was signed between Mauritania and the POLISARIO Front. The war now revealed the two main antagonists—Morocco and Algeria, who for the next decade until the normalization of relations between them in 1988 cut off support for the rebels, fought for ultimate control of the region. In 1991 a cease-fire was agreed between Morocco and the POLISARIO Front and another UN-sponsored referendum was recommended and delayed, during which time the region was to all intents and purposes integrated into Morocco.

List of participants:...	POLISARIO Front, FLU, PUNS, Morocco, Algeria, Mauritania
Duration:...............	1976–91
Location:...............	Spanish Sahara
Outcome:...............	Integrated into Morocco
Casualty figures:.......	20,000

Gen. Ne Wine (center), chairman of Burma's ruling Revolutionary council, is accompanied by President Lyndon Johnson as he salutes the colors during a review of the honor guard upon his arrival at the White House.

1948–

Burma has eight major ethnic groups—Burmans (the largest and most dominant), Shans, Kachins, Karens, Karenni, Mons, Chins, and Arakans—who were all separate tribal kingdoms until the British took over the area. No sooner had they been granted independence as the Union of Federated States of Burma in 1948, than they began to disintegrate back into their original groups.

To begin with a vicious war broke out between the government and the Burmese Communist Party (CPB) in many areas. Other Chinese Kuomintang survivors (CIF) also fled over the border from their defeat in China in a sizable numbers. This was followed almost immediately by a Karen insurrection in 1949. The Burman federal government couldn't cope with so much simultaneous fragmentation, and soon almost 40 percent of the country was held by insurgents of one sort or another.

In 1962 the Burma Army's Chief Commander, General Ne Win, took advantage of the chaos to stage a military coup. Once in power, he set about regaining control of the country using the pretext of claiming to safeguard the possible disintegration of the union to systematically attack all ethnic groups. By isolating Burma from the rest of the world, he was able to suppress all freedom of expression and association, repress all other political organizations, and institute draconian economic and human rights policies. In this fashion he created an enemy out of all non-Burman tribal groups and drove them to military resistance by exploiting the political unrest, which could be used to justify military intervention on the government's part. As any kind of fabric of a normal society was stripped away, people were brutalized by endless atrocities.

Syriam, Burma: Anti Chinese Demonstration. A group of students and other Burmese burns the "coffin" of Chairman Mao Tse Tung, during an anti-Communist Chinese demonstration here recently. Such mass protests are reported to be taking place in various parts of the country. According to Peking's New China News Agency, Communist china demanded an immediate halt to all anti-Chinese activities in Burma.

This time also saw the growth of warlords with no political agenda other than profit—in an area known as the Golden Triangle which has become one of the world's centers of opium/heroin production and continues to finance the warfare, with the collusion of the cash-hungry central government. The result was bitter fighting that continues to this day.

List of participants:...Burman majority government under military, CPB, CIF, tribal resistance groups, warlords.
Duration:.................1948–
Location:..................Burma
Outcome:..................Ongoing
Casualty figures:.......Ongoing

Arab "Green Helmet" troops take position in Beirut, waiting to control the nearby cities of Saida and Tyr.

1958–

U ntil 1864 Lebanon was part of the Syrian province of the Ottoman Empire. The area then fell under French control, and in 1920 France created the current Lebanon by combining Christian areas in the west with Muslim territories to the north, east, and south. In 1946 Lebanon became independent for the first time in its history, on the basis of a power-sharing between Muslims and Christians, who formed almost equal proportions of the population. However, this was an impossible dream for a Middle Eastern country given the time and the place. For a brief honeymoon period Lebanon shone as an example to all, but by the 1950s the cracks were already beginning to appear as the inevitable tensions between Christians and Muslims increased. The Christian President Chamoun's pro-western support of the Suez crisis incensed Arab nationalists, and in May 1958 the Muslims in Tripoli, Beirut, Sidon, and the Shi'ite region of Baalbek rose in revolt, with the Syrians taking over border areas in support of the rebellion. President Chamoun appealed directly to the U.S. who sent troops to the capital Beirut in July.

In September with a change of president the trouble seemed to die down and U.S. forces were withdrawn by the end of the year. However, the troubles between Israel and its Arab neighbors meant that the peace didn't last long, and an influx of over 200,000 Palestinian refugees didn't make matters any easier. Civil war broke out again in April 1975, between the right-wing Christian Phalangist party and left-wing Muslim groups. Heavy Israeli raids on South Lebanon in retaliation for Palestinian guerrilla attacks caused still more extensive destruction and disruption. Sectarian fighting began in Tripoli in mid-March and spread to Beirut in April. In May and June new governments were formed and folded, incapable of solving the crisis. In 1976 there was countrywide fighting when Phalangist right-wing Christian forces blockaded

Soldiers, under Major Haddad, stand beside Sherman and French AMX military tanks outside the SL Militia headquarters. The tanks were supplied by their Israeli allies.

Palestinian refugee camps. The Palestinians retaliated by laying siege to Christian villages. By June Syrian troops entered the fray with their first large-scale intervention, advancing as far as the Bekaa Valley, which they occupied after a fierce struggle with the PLO. Finally a cease-fire was agreed at Riyadh on October 17 between the leaders of Saudi Arabia, Syria, Egypt, Lebanon, and the PLO. It was policed by the newly formed Arab Deterrent Forces (ADF), composed mainly of Syrian troops. This ended 19 months of civil war which had killed over 45,000, wounded 100,000 and forced another 500,000 to emigrate.

The next year fierce fighting between Christian rightists and Palestinians erupted again in February around Marjayoun and continued throughout the summer. Israel supported the Christians with artillery and armor. The assassination of the Druze leader, Kamal Jumblatt, on March 16 was followed by Druze attacks on Christian villages and the inevitable reprisals. With the Israeli 1982 invasion, Lebanon slipped into anarchy, the divide between the various elements too great for it to survive with the wider ongoing Middle East crisis, for its fate is tied to the intrinsic problems shared by the whole region.

List of participants:... Maronite and Falange Christian, Druze, Shi'ite and Sunni Muslims, Israel, PLO, Syria, U.S.
Duration:................ 1958–
Location:................. Lebanon
Outcome:................ Ongoing
Casualty figures:....... Ongoing

Military convoy of the Indonesian army in the streets of Dili, East Timor.

1975–76

In colonial times the island of Timor was divided between the Portuguese and the Dutch. The Dutch western side became a part of Indonesia in 1950, but the Portuguese were loath to give up their part and as a result unrest began to spread. There were three main groups fighting for independence—on the nationalist side were the Timor Democratic Union (UDT) and the Timorese Democratic People's Union (APODETI), and on the communist side the Revolutionary Front for Independence (FREITLIN).

In 1975 Portugal had finally given up her African possessions and the writing was on the wall for Portuguese East Timor. In August that year the UDT attacked a government police headquarters and kidnapped the chief of police. Their demands were for immediate independence and the imprisonment of all members of FREITLIN: as a result by late August 20 full-scale civil war broke out between these nationalist and communist groups. Initially FREITLIN gained the upper hand, and by September claimed to control the whole country, with over 50,000 refugees fleeing the violence. FREITLIN then began to launch incursions into West Timor and was threatened with retaliation by Indonesia. At the end of November FREITLIN proclaimed East Timor an independent democratic republic but this was followed promptly by an Indonesian invasion in the first week of December. 1,000 paratroopers seized Dili and expelled the FREITLIN who dispersed into the hills. The Indonesians then went on to take Maubara and Baucau, enabling the UDT and APODETI to set up a provisional government. In July 1976, Portuguese Timor was officially integrated into Indonesia, although the problems in East Timor persist.

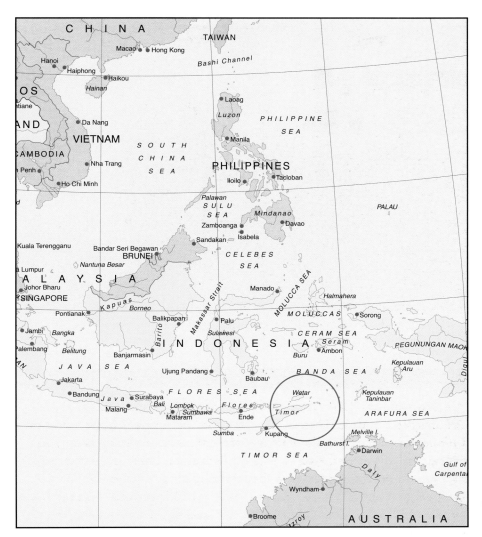

List of participants:... UDT, APODETI, FREITLIN
Duration:................ 1975–76
Location:................ Timor
Outcome:................ East Timor integrated into Indonesia
Casualty figures: 100,000

*Cuban President Fidel Castro is flanked by Leabua Jonathan, Prime Minister of Lesotho (l)
and Samora Moises Machel, President of Mozambique, on their arrival 9/1 for a summit of
Non-Aligned Nations.*

1964–94

Mozambique has over 20 different tribal and ethnic groups. In
1505, the Portuguese made the area their primary trade center on
the eastern coast of Africa, remorselessly denuding it of manpower (as
slaves) and any other resources it possessed, while putting nothing back.
By 1962 an independence movement was finally formed—the Front
for the Liberation of Mozambique (FRELIMO) led by Dr. Eduardo
Mondlane. It had its headquarters in Dar-es-Salaam and enjoyed the full
support of Tanzania, who provided its main training base at Nachingwea.
FRELIMO also received generous advice and supplies from China. In the
autumn of 1964 FRELIMO began a savage ten-year war of independence
against the Portuguese. In 1970 the FRELIMO leadership passed to
Samora Machel, a particularly hard-line Marxist, who began a new
offensive in the Tete area, particularly around the sensitive Cabora-Bassa
dam site. In 1972 December an international outcry followed after the
massacre of 300–400 villagers in the settlements of Wiryamu, Chawda
and Juwau near Tete by black Portuguese troops. In September 1974
rumors of an impending agreement between Portugal and FRELIMO
lead to short-lived revolt of despair by white Mozambicans and pro-
Portuguese blacks in Lourengo Marques. The retaliatory pro-FRELIMO
backlash took over 9,500 lives. However, in early 1975 with the change
of government in Portugal came a change in approach. On September
7 the Portuguese Foreign Minister signed the Lusaka Agreement with
Samora Machel, proclaiming a cease-fire and on July 25, 1975, Machel
proclaimed the independence of the People's Republic of Mozambique.

Since its independence in 1975 Mozambique has faced continued
civil war. In the 1970s Rhodesia (now Zimbabwe) and South Africa were
both ruled by white minority governments hostile to Mozambique's
new government, both of whom helped subsidize the creation of an

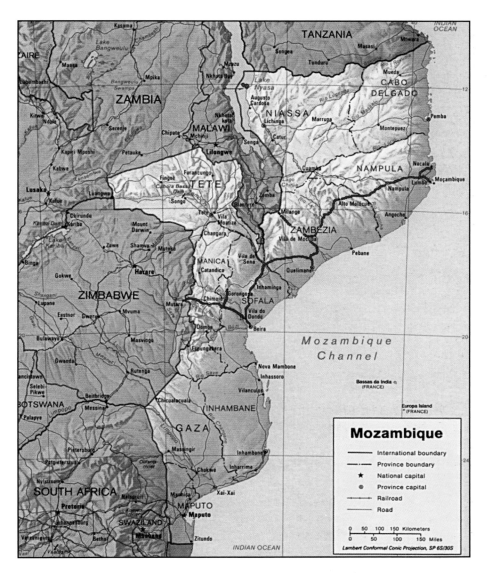

anti-FRELIMO army called the Mozambican National Resistance (RENAMO).

The ensuing 15 year war between FRELIMO and RENAMO was devastating for the country, with an estimated million people killed and over three times that refugees. Mozambique's infrastructure and economy were destroyed and the initial optimism of independence died in the hunger and destruction. Recent events give cause for fragile hope. In 1992 FRELIMO and RENAMO forces ended their civil war and signed peace accords. In 1994 both parties participated in Mozambique's first multiparty elections and reelected FRELIMO led by Joaquim Alberto Chissano. Also, Mozambique's neighbors are now more friendly after to the fall of the white minority governments in South Africa and Rhodesia.

List of participants:... Portugal, FRELIMO, RENAMO
Duration:................. 1964–94
Location:.................. Mozambique
Outcome:.................. Independence and eventual peace
Casualty figures:....... Over one million

Namibian men hold their country's flag during their independence celebration.

1966–90

South Africa first occupied Namibia in 1915 and in 1920 had its mandate confirmed by the League of Nations. At the end of World War II, the newly formed United Nations attempted to make South Africa reconsider its position and accept that it had only been given trustee status for that territory, but the South African government refused to budge, insisting that it was the sovereign power. It suited the apartheid regime to have Namibia under its control to act as a buffer state. Throughout the 1950s the South African government continued to try and incorporate Namibia more fully into its territory, which in turn stimulated the formation of an independence movement. In 1960 the South West Africa People's Organization (SWAPO) was formed and by 1966 was actively involved in an armed struggle. South Africa proclaimed Ovamboland as Namibia's first homeland in 1967, and Namibia was then virtually made into a province. In 1968 the country was renamed Namibia by the UN and external pressure continued to be put on the South African minority white government. SWAPO's leaders were soon forced into exile in Zambia and Angola, where they established bases from which to continue the guerrilla war, backed by Angola and the Soviet Union. The UN also continued to pressure South Africa to change its policy—still to no avail—attempts to implement Apartheid protocols continued during the 1970s. In 1971 the UN General Assembly, keeping up the pressure, recognized SWAPO as the sole legitimate representative of the Namibian people and the group was still further strengthened when Angola became independent from Portugal in 1975. South Africa responded by giving aid to the pro-Western UNITA group and tried to bring down the Marxist Angolan government and this conflict also crossed the border into Namibia during the 1970s. Finally after years of delays and prevarication and under continuous international pressure, South Africa entered negotiations with SWAPO in 1984. Wily as ever

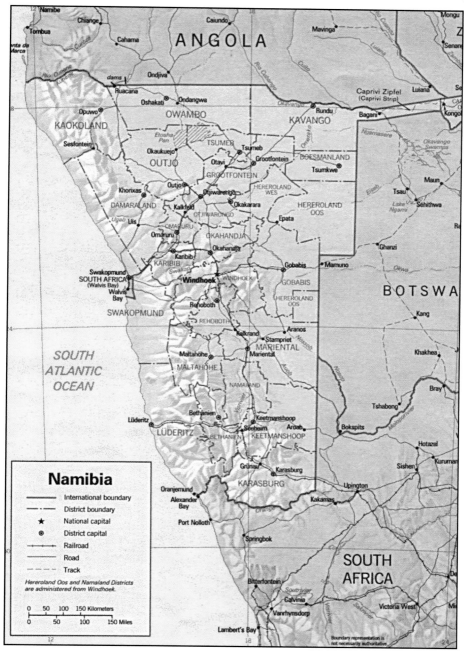

and mindful of their security, they linked the Namibia issue to the continued existence of Cuban troops in Angola and they formed a new multi-racial government in 1985 which was discredited and discounted by SWAPO. Finally in 1988 an agreement was reached and both South Africa and Angola withdrew from Namibia. In April 1989, a UN peace-keeping force arrived and Namibia finally shook off the last vestiges of South African domination in 1990. Independence followed in 2002.

List of participants:... SWAPO, South Africa
Duration:................. 1966–90
Location:................. Namibia
Outcome:................. Independence
Casualty figures: 40,000

A crowd gathers for the funeral of United Democratic Front leader Peter Nchabeleng, who was murdered while imprisoned for his anti-apartheid actions.

1910–89

Emerging from the chaos of the Boer War, the Union of South Africa was set up in 1910, and by passing many blatantly racist laws maintained the exclusive political control that had always been enjoyed by the white minority—whether Boer or British. During this time the Afrikaans concept of apartheid was developed: whereby the races were kept completely segregated. In 1948 the Afrikaans National Party came to power and set about realizing its apartheid policy of separate development by enacting legislation that excluded blacks and coloreds from having any political or economic influence whatsoever. With the passing of these apartheid laws, racial discrimination became systematically institutionalized and impinged on every aspect of life, from the prohibition of any mixed-race marriages to housing, education, and employment. Next came the 1950 Population Registration Act, which required all South Africans to be racially classified into one of three categories: white, black (African), or brown (colored, Indian, Asian or of mixed parentage). Needless to say this outrageous legislation succeeded in polarizing opinion and in aiding the formation of the African National Congress (ANC)—to campaign for black and colored rights. The ANC began by protesting peacefully and was either ignored or imprisoned, so it stepped up the pace and began a violent guerrilla war, supported by neighboring black nationalist states. The government responded by declaring a state of emergency, activating its secret police, its paramilitary police, and the army. Thousands were spied upon, set up, arrested, and tortured. Many died in custody, while others who stood trial were sentenced to death, banished or imprisoned for life. Throughout the 1960s many of the leaders of the ANC were picked off—either murdered or imprisoned. One of the many arrested and jailed was the future President Nelson Mandela.

Anti-apartheid activist Nelson Mandela shortly after his release from a South African prison in 1990. He had been imprisoned for his anti-apartheid activities for nearly 25 years.

In the 1970s the government began a new tactic by creating "black homelands," ostensibly to give tribal areas autonomy, but in reality to turn all blacks who entered designated white areas into aliens with no rights. By the late 1970s many neighboring countries had Marxist governments backed by the USSR. This made the white South African minority even more aggressive and thinking its best form of defense was attack it invaded southern Angola. Despite Cold War considerations and partly because of South Africa's extraordinary mineral resources as well as the growing popular protest in their own countries, the west felt obliged to put pressure on the white minority government. This rising protest was augmented in the early 1980s when both the Commonwealth and the UN demanded political and economic sanctions against the regime. As outside pressure mounted, the white minority government was constrained to make concessions, thereby arousing the ire of their own hardcore right wing. But the pressure for a genuine majority rule democracy was inexorable and in 1989 the South African President F.W. de Klerk began the process of reform. The next year peace was negotiated with the ANC and Nelson Mandela was released. A referendum held in 1991 overwhelmingly voted in favor of continuing along the road to a true democracy and in 1994 Nelson Mandela was momentously elected as president.

List of participants:... South African white government, ANC
Duration:................. 1910–89
Location:................. South Africa
Outcome:................. Majority rule democracy
Casualty figures: 500,000

The leaders of the Southern Sudan Factions shake hands with the help of Emperor Haile Selassie.

1955–89

Sudan is essentially split between the Arab Muslim north and Bantu Christian and pagan south. This antagonism goes back a long way—into the days when the coastal Arabs were slavers who exploited the south. When the British took over the Sudan they had a policy of keeping the two elements apart and the country was ruled jointly by Britain and Egypt after the defeat of the Khalifa in 1899 until 1953 when it was granted self-government. Independence followed in 1956—by which time fighting had already broken out between the north and south. The radical Arab National Unionist Party (NUP) was campaigning for Sudanese-Egyptian unification. The more moderate Umma Party preferred independence through cooperation with Britain. However, the NUP won the elections and its leader Ismail al-Aihari, became the Sudan's first Prime Minister in January 1954. British and Egyptians in the Sudanese civil service and government were soon replaced almost exclusively by Arab northerners.

Unhappy with this state of affairs protests escalated in the south and on July 26, 1955, eight people were killed in Nzara when two northern merchants fired into a crowd of southerners. By August there had been a mutiny of southern troops at Torit in which almost 300 northerners were massacred. This brought prolonged and shocking retribution from the north as the civil war picked up pace. In November 17, 1958, General Ibrahim Abboud toppled the government of al-Azharia in a bloodless army coup and the northern-dominated military took over. In 1963, primarily as a defense against savage northern attacks and reprisals, southerners formed the Anya-Nya guerrilla force under the leadership of General Joseph Lagu. By 1966 the security situation in the southern Sudan had become serious. Despite ministerial visits and attempts at dialog the rebels would not yield, so in October 1970 the government launched a major military campaign over the next two years in order to subdue them.

The civil war ended officially in March 1972, when a peace accord was signed with the Anya-Nya rebels in the south. However four

years later there was another coup attempted by exiled members of
the previous government—2,000 heavily armed supporters stormed
into Khartoum and Omdurman, causing massive destruction before
being neutralized. Almost 100 were executed and several hundred were
imprisoned. This attempted coup had the effect of bringing Sudan closer
to its two most powerful neighbors, Egypt and Saudi Arabia. From
1982 a tide of refugees from neighboring conflicts began to seep into
the country—by 1985 it had become a flood of over a million, with the
numbers still growing. At this time, in 1983 the penal code was changed
to Islamic Sharia Law. This had the effect of alienating the Christian
and pagan south again and a new group—the Southern Sudan People's
Liberation Army (SPLA) began to spread from its base in the Upper
Nile and the Bahr El Ghazal region. In 1985, with growing discontent
and huge numbers of refugees, there was yet another military coup. The
conditions in the country then destabilized sufficiently to spark a whole
series of coups and countercoups. Finally in 1989 the army stepped in
again, suspending the normal political processes that had broken down.
There then followed almost five years of military rule until it was felt that
stability had been restored and a new civilian government was formed.

List of participants:... NUP, Umma, Anya-Nya, SPLA
Duration:................. 1955–89
Location:.................. Sudan
Outcome:.................. Military rule
Casualty figures:....... 1,000,000

A Somalian soldier lies low in a trench on the front line opposite Ethiopian enemy territory situated 500m on the other side.

1974–

The Ogaden was an independent country of a Somalian people until the technologically superior Europeans divided up Africa. It was then absorbed into neighboring Abyssinia, whose territorial ambitions were expanding in collusion with the British. In 1948 Abyssinia renamed itself Ethiopia and began to escalate the war against the separationist Ogaden Somalis. In 1960 the Somali Democratic Republic came into being, intent on regaining the Ogaden. In 1974 a Somali-backed nationalist guerrilla movement—the Western Somalia Liberation Front (WSLF)—emerged to fight against Ethiopian domination and recover lost territories.

With the downfall of Haile Selassie in September 1974 and the ensuing chaos in Ethiopia until the Dergue—the new government—took hold, Somalia took the opportunity to increase its support for the WSLF with troops from its own Somalian National Army (SNA). By 1977 the combined WSLF-SNA strength in the Ogaden was around 50,000 and this escalated the conflict from a hit-and-run guerrilla campaign to a conventional all-arms war in which armor, mechanized infantry, and air power all played key roles. In the summer of 1977 the war began in earnest, with the SNA-WSLF capturing Gode—over 300 miles inside Ethiopian territory. By the middle of that year, Ethiopia conceded that most of the Ogaden was in Somali hands. However, when they attempted to take Dire Dawa and Jijiga they were repulsed with heavy losses. In the second attempt to take Jijiga they overwhelmed the garrison and pushed the Ethiopians back to the Marda Pass.

This was the high watermark of the SNA-WSLF campaign, for a combination of military and political factors now changed the situation. In the military sphere the Somalis, having advanced so far, had vulnerable

Western Somalia Liberation Front guerillas train at a military camp in Somalia. The struggle continues with Ethiopians for the control of Ogaden, and the Somalian government turns a blind eye to the theft of nutritional aid packages sent to the refugee camps in Somalia from overseas.

extended supply lines—and the Ethiopians had recently won air superiority. More important, in the political sphere the USSR, who had been supplying both countries with arms, abandoned Somalia in favor of Ethiopia. Although the SNA-WSLF continued with its offensive into early 1978, the Ethiopians held their line until substantially reequipped. Then, with an army twice the size of its opponent, complete with 10,000 Cuban and 2,000 Russian "advisers" launched a counterattack. Within a single week the Ethiopians had retaken all of the Ogaden's major towns and the SNA went home. Once again the war became a guerrilla campaign for the WSLF—who modified its name to the Ogadenia National Liberation Front (ONLF) and throughout the 1980s continued to fight tenaciously, winning back a significant portion of the Ogaden. In 1994 the UN and the Organization of African Unity restated the desire for a referendum, but the Ethiopians promptly launched a massive offensive against the ONLF. The situation is currently unresolved and still ongoing.

List of participants:... WSLF-ONLF, SNA, Ethiopia
Duration:................. 1974–
Location:................. Ogaden, Somalia, Ethiopia
Outcome:................. Ongoing
Casualty figures: .... 250,000 and ongoing

1979–89

Afghanistan is a wild mountainous country without much infrastructure, which makes communication and traveling difficult, peopled with over ten different ethnic and tribal groups, the largest of which are the Pashtun. The population for the most part are rural, deeply conservative, and traditional Muslims. In the social and political changes of the 1970s an indigenous town-based communist party overthrew the Afghan monarchy and tried to introduce reforms including land redistribution and women's rights—without much success. Soviet aid began at this time, with roads and irrigation projects, schools as well as political and military advisers.

January 1979 saw the Shah overthrown in neighboring Iran as the resurgence of Islamic fundamentalism started. Soon most of the Afghan provinces were in open revolt, and as it became more beleaguered the communist government appealed for increased Soviet military aid. Driven by geo-political considerations and mindful of their own large Muslim populations of Soviet Central Asia, the Soviets saw a way to expand their influence in the area. In December the Russian Army went over the border with over 100,000 troops, quickly securing Kabul and installed Babrak Karmal as the new head of government.

However, when they ventured out into the countryside they encountered fierce opposition. The Muslim Afghan fighters were

Night Battle in Soviet-Afghan War.

Nuristani Afghan rebels standing on a captured Russian helicopter during the Soviet-Afghan war.

The first major attack on Kabul by mujahideen belonging to Mahaz-e-Melli.

united enough by this outside invader with an alien ideology, burying underlying tribal tensions and calling themselves Mujahadin, they declared a jihad or Holy War against the Russians, and began a guerrilla war that ideally suited both the terrain and their nature. The USSR's invasion also drew strong reaction from all over the world. The United States immediately began supplying extensive military aid and food to the Mujahadin. The UN condemned Soviet aggression and demanded that they pull out immediately. The Arab world, too, began to supply money, weapons, and volunteers to the Mujahadin. This continuous and ample supply of military and financial aid balanced the numerical superiority and firepower of the Soviets. These efforts also soon had an effect on the nature of the war—western handheld missiles such as the U.S. Stinger and British Blowpipe brought down many Russian helicopters and aircraft, forcing Soviet air cover higher. The Soviet-held towns began to be hemmed-in and their supply convoys continuously attacked. The viciousness of this war was apparent with no quarter given by either side. As the Mujahadin grew more confident they began to attack the towns and cities as well, and the Russians were forced completely onto the defensive. Having spent billions in pursuit of impractical military dreams, the strain on the Soviet system was so intense it now began to unravel. In 1989, Soviet forces pulled out of Afghanistan, having incurred over 15,000 casualties. In 1994 a new ultra-religious Muslim group emerged—the Taliban—serious hardcore extremists opposed to all modern inventions other than weaponry. By 1996 they controlled most of the country..

List of participants:... USSR, Mujahadin, Taliban
Duration:............... 1979–89
Location:.................. Afghanistan
Outcome:................ Ejection of USSR, emergence of Taliban
Casualty figures: 100,000

Afghan Soldiers Sitting on Armored Military Vehicles.

Ayatollah Ruhollah Khomeini, 78, exiled leader of the Iranian Shi-ite Muslims, at prayers at his temporary refuge at Neauphle-le Chateau, 25 miles from Paris. The Ayatollah opposes the Shah of Iran in favour of an "Islamic Republic".

1974-78

On September 16, 1941, during World War II, Mohammad Reza Shah Pahlavi succeeded to the throne as the Shah of Iran—a throne that had been usurped by his army officer father in 1921 and who had been deposed by Britain and U.S. because of the threat to their Iranian oilfields and his refusal to expel German oil advisers. Postwar, although he promised to continue with his father's reforms and defer to the parliamentary government, in fact the Shah had his own agenda—to safeguard and increase his own personal power, and to this end he tried to manipulate the politicians.

However, thwarted by strong political leaders and a lively political process, he turned instead to the military. Ensuring that it remained under royal control, he concentrated on building it up as his primary powerbase. In 1949 he took advantage of an assassination attempt to insist that the communist Tudeh party was proscribed. Even though his father had attempted to undermine the strong U.S. and British oil interests in the country, Iran needed western technology in order to develop its infrastructure, so the Shah now made himself a vital ally of the west in the Cold War, while making the most of the opportunity to further build up his armed forces. His domestic reforms were an attempt to modernize Iran, but aside from the ruling classes the vast bulk of the population was living a life not much changed for a thousand years, and his policies threatened traditional authority and religious values. The massive discrepancy in wealth and distribution of resources continued to exert inexorable pressure. In the face of increasing criticism and protest the Shah turned to the Savak—Iran's internal security and intelligence organization—whose methods of repression included violence and torture.

In 1979, The Shah of Iran flees into exile and his country is taken over by Right wing religeous fundamentalists.

Using the revenues generated from oil the Shah attempted to build Iran into a local regional superpower, but increasingly there was no room for opposition or debate. By the mid-1970s the gap between those who prospered under his regime and the majority of the population was so large that Muslim clerics—the focus of the opposition—were able to harness the resulting discontent into an Islamic revolution. Protest and riots became still more widespread in 1978 and the following year elements of the military began to join the protesters and the Shah's government collapsed. Broken and ill, with not much longer to live, he fled into exile, to be succeeded by a revolutionary Islamic government headed by the Grand Ayatollah Khomeini, triumphantly returned from exile.

List of participants:... Shah, Khomeini—the monarchy v fundamentalist Islam
Duration: 1974-78
Location: .... Iran
Outcome: .... Overthrow of the Shah, ascendance of Ayatollah Khomeini
Casualty figures: 100,000

The first Chinese prisoners-of-war paraded by the Vietnamese, before foreign newsmen at Pho Lu regional military headquarters, 12 miles south of the Chinese border. The prisoners are Teng Fei Lin, (foreground), a tank driver, and Wu Sun Tao, a guide.

FEBRUARY-MARCH 1979

On February 17, 1979, 70-80,000 Chinese troops stormed over the border into Vietnam across a wide front in six main thrusts aimed primarily at major northern towns and cities. This Chinese attack was in retaliation for a combination of reasons that—in Chinese eyes—made it absolutely necessary: Vietnam's invasion and occupation of Cambodia, the overthrow of the Chinese-supported Khmer Rouge regime, and the mistreatment of the 1.5-million Chinese minority in Vietnam. China was not best pleased with its neighbor and wished to reassert its authority. Cam Duong fell on the day of the invasion, Lao Kay on the 19th, and Cao Bang and Ha Giang on the 22nd.

The Vietnamese rushed 50,000 troops northward to stem the advance, but the Chinese brought in reinforcements of their own to bring their numbers up to over 200,000 men and resumed the offensive. On March 2 they took Lang Son after a heavy fight—Vietnamese resistance was stiffening considerably as they, too, brought more soldiers into the conflict. On March 5. Peking suddenly announced that their troops had accomplished everything they set out to do and recalled them. As they withdrew they were harried and harassed by the Vietnamese— with more intense fighting around the Lang Son area. On March 17, the Chinese announced that all troops had left Vietnam. Both sides then claimed to be the victors of this brief encounter.

The Chinese had obliterated four provincial capitals in the north of the country and given the Soviet-supported Vietnamese a bloody nose for what it saw as getting above its station. The Vietnamese were determined to ignore this and continued expending valuable resources on the what they considered to be well worthwhile—controlling and fragmenting the hated Khmer as much as they possibly could.

Lang Son, Vietnam: Scattered Vietnamese people cross the Ky Cuong River on temporary floating bridge as several hundred residents have returned to this rubbled village to try to pick up at least part of their lives shattered by the Chinese invasion which began Feb. 17 and Lang Son was the main target of the four-week invasion. The Ky Lua Bridge at right lies in ruins although a few installations are being repaired.

List of participants:... China, Vietnam
Duration:................. February-March 1979
Location:.................. Vietnam
Outcome:................. Punitive raid, four regional capitals trashed
Casualty figures: 20-30,000

Managua, Nicaragua: Daniel Ortega (L), member of Nicaragua's junta, leads thousands of Nicaraguans through the streets of the capital in demonstration of support for the new Sandinista government.

1978–95

Nicaragua is another central South American nation which has cause to regret its proximity to a powerful neighbor, for having won its independence from Spain in 1821, it was then occupied militarily to act as a buffer state to protect the Panama Canal. Colluding with the U.S. was the small ruling elite (10 percent) of landowners. When the U.S. left in 1925, it took less than a decade before power in Nicaragua was seized by a single infamous dynasty—the Somozas, who first took control in 1933 with the aid of the National Guard.

The Somoza regime began to industrialize Nicaragua rapidly, encouraging a rural exodus to the cities to serve this purpose, and at the same time leave large amounts of agricultural land to turn into huge private plantations. However, there was little or no provision for the workers themselves—the infrastructure was privately owned, unions were forbidden, and the wealth did not percolate down through society. In the early 1970s two critical events then occurred which were to make matters much worse—the world oil crisis that plunged Nicaragua's economy into chaos, and in 1972 a massive earthquake which destroyed much of the capital, Managua. In spite of international aid, Somoza's government did not repair the destruction, and unrest began to pick up pace.

Open rebellion erupted in 1978 soon after the most serious opponent of President Somoza, Pedro Joaquin Chamorro Cardenal, was assassinated. A guerilla movement—the Frente Sandinista de Liberacion Nacional (FSLN)—emerged to take on the regime's military. Within a year things had deteriorated to such an extent that the U.S. encouraged Somoza to flee so that a more moderate government could be installed. In 1984 national elections were held and Daniel Ortega Saavedra, the Sandinista presidential candidate, won by an overwhelming

Troops from the Sandinista Peoples' Army climb aboard a Soviet-made helicopter in the northern mountains of Nicaragua.

majority. At first the Sandinista communists were a success but with their nationalization program of land and private industry and the redistribution of private property they alienated both the middle class and the rural poor.

The U.S. stepped up its military and financial aid to the Contras while imposing an embargo and sanctions on the beleaguered country. When the Sandinista government lost Russian support, as the U.S.S.R. itself slipped into crisis, things began to fall to pieces. By March 1988 the pressure told and the Sandinistas were forced into peace talks with the Contras. In 1990 fresh elections removed the Sandinistas and a U.S.-backed party—the National Opposition Union (UNO)—won a majority and installed a new president. However Ortega remained as the Army Chief and thus war continued between the Sandinistas and Contras until he stepped down peaceably in 1995.

List of participants:... U.S., Somoza, FSLN, CONTRA, UNO
Duration:................. 1978–95
Location:.................. Nicaragua
Outcome:................. Somoza out, then the Sandinistas voted out
Casualty figures: 25,000

Photo shows Hostages photographed inside the United States embassy compound as they are led outside the building, blindfolded on the first day of the occupation.

1979–80

Iran's dislike of the U.S. has roots that go back to the discovery of oil in the country. Along with Britain, the U.S. owned extensive oilfields and therefore supported and maintained the regime of the Shah, helping him build up his army and even having the CIA train his security organization Savak. Apart from the westernized ruling elite, the rest of the people were Shia Muslims living pretty much as they always had done, for few of the oil profits ever reached the populace.

Opposition to the Shah was mainly in the hands of religious leaders, rather than the suppressed Iranian communist party the Tudeh. Protests brutally suppressed under martial law inevitably led to increased resistance and armed insurrection. Finally, in 1979, a fundamentalist Islamic revolution overthrew the Shah and he fled, leaving the country in the hands of its new ruler, the Ayatollah Khomeini.

While still in the early throes of jubilation, rage had also been compounded by the exiled Shah of Iran's admission to the U.S. for medical treatment and the freezing of Iranian assets in U.S. banks. On November 4 of that same revolutionary year, a crowd of about 500 radical students and militants seized the U.S. embassy in the capital Tehran, taking almost 100 hostages including around 60 Americans. They were then held in the longest siege of modern history—a total of 444 days, in spite of international condemnation.

Matters were made worse by an abortive rescue attempt by the U.S. military. The embassy's papers had been found intact, implicating many Iranian politicians and others in dealing with the Americans—all of whom were executed.

Robat-e Posht-e Badam, Iran: Miscellaneous view of wreckage from aborted attempt to rescue U. S. Embassy hostages in Tehran.

In July 1980 the Shah died in exile and the release of the hostages was expertly timed to coincide with the day of President Reagan's inauguration, and the U.S. release of almost $8 billion of Iranian assets.

Less than two years later, after a series of bloody purges, the revolution that had promised so much had become as brutal and reactionary as that of the Shah.

List of participants:... Iran, U.S.
Duration:.................444 days 1979–80
Location:................. Tehran, Iran
Outcome:................. Eventual release of hostages
Casualty figures: 1,000

An Iraqi tank on the front 100 kms from Basra in the Alhoueiza swamp region near the village of Al Azayr. Meanwhile in the north the Iranian Army have just crossed the river Tigris.

1980–88

Iraq and Iran had engaged in border clashes and disputes over the Shatt al Arab waterway for many years, fueled by Sunni-Shia and Arab-Persian religious and ethnic divides. On September 22, 1980, Iraqi president Saddam Hussein, fearing the spread of Iran's Shia Islamic revolution to Iraq's majority Shia population and aware of the degradation of Iran's military through brutal purges, ordered the invasion of Iran.

There was also a great deal of personal animosity between the two leaders for the Iranian Ayatollah Khomeini, had been expelled from Iraq in 1977 after 15 years' exile in Najaf and he had vowed to avenge all the Shia victims of Saddam's repressive Baathist regime. Iraq, having been recently reequipped by the USSR, was bristling with equipment and troops. Iran's armed forces, on the other hand, were led by mullahs with little military experience. The initial Iraqi assault against scattered disorganized forces was almost completely successful—capturing the Shatt al Arab and penetrating deep into Iranian territory. However, the expected victory didn't happen and Iranian resistance did not crumble— on the contrary it hardened into a fanatical religious crusade. By the end of the following year the advantage had turned in Iran's favor, and in 1982 they launched an invasion into Iraq. This, too, ended in a stalemate and the war soon settled into one of attrition.

Both sides used their Kurdish minorities from which to launch attacks on the other, and both air forces were some of the best assets each side possessed, bombing oil installations, tankers, fuel dumps, and command/control centers as well as cities and civilians.

An Iraqi artillery batallion situated in the Maysan sector to the east of Amara in action.

Guided missiles were also a feature of this war, targeting civilians in a phase called the War of the Cities. From 1982 until 1987 Iran had the initiative and Iraq was on the defensive; however, the Iraqis made up for their smaller numbers with a technological edge that cancelled out Iran's numerical advantage. By 1987 both sides were worn out and though their hatred hadn't dimmed certainly their armies and people were exhausted by almost a decade of bitter war. In 1988 a UN brokered cease-fire was agreed.

List of participants:... Iran, Iraq
Duration:................. 1980–88
Location:................. Iran, Iraq
Outcome:................. Stalemate
Casualty figures: 600,000

Undated police hand-out of a Red Army Fraction member wanted list. Upper row left-right: Andreas Baader, Ulrike Meinhof, Gudrun Ensslin and Ronald Augustin. Below left-right: Jan-Carl Raspe, Klaus Juenschke, Ilse Stachowiak und Irmgard Mueller.

1960s–1998

The origins of the Red Army Faction, also known as the Baader Meinhof gang or group, can be traced back to the student demonstrations in the turbulent 1960s, when a protest turned into a riot in which a German student was shot by an over-reactive policeman. This and other brutal suppressions of student demonstrations brought Thorwald Proll, Horst Stein, Gudrun Ensslin, and Andreas Baader together to form a group to retaliate against the state. In their first reprisal, they firebombed various German department stores—and were promptly caught. Some went on the run, but others were tried, and Baader was imprisoned, to be freed later in a daring armed rescue.

The group then went underground and traveled to Jordan to receive military and terrorist training. When they returned to West Germany, they launched another anti-capitalist campaign, financed in classic fashion with kidnappings and bank robberies. Targets included U.S. military facilities, German police stations, and large corporations. At this time a manifesto issued by the group used the Red Army Faction (RAF) name and logo—a red star surmounted by a machine gun. Finally, after an intensive security operation, they were all caught in 1972 and jailed separately. In 1974, protesting at their isolation, one of them died on hunger strike and as a result their conditions were slightly improved. Early in 1975 a second version of RAF appeared, consisting of members sympathetic to but unconnected with the original group. They kidnapped one of the candidates in the Berlin mayoral elections and traded him with the government for several detained terrorists—though none of the original RAF were released. On May 21, 1975, these original members began their lengthy trial. A year later, while it was still going on, Ulrike Meinhof was found hanged in her cell, which sparked off many conspiracy theories. With the trial still ongoing on April 7, 1977,

One of the leaders of the infamous Baader-Meinhof Gang of Terrorists is arrested in London. Astrid Proll, 32.

the Federal Prosecutor and his chauffeur were shot at a red traffic light by the new RAF. At the end of May the three original RAF defendants were convicted and sentenced to life imprisonment. A third generation RAF later surfaced in the early 1980s and continued to assassinate leading businessmen, industrialists, and executives and to target U.S. installations. After the reunification of Germany in 1990, it was revealed that RAF had been financed and equipped by the East German security and intelligence organization Stasi, and information from their files lead to a further arrests as these terrorists were hunted down. On April 20, 1998, Reuters received a document purporting to be from RAF declaring the organization dissolved.

List of participants:... RAF, German government
Duration:................ 1960s–1998
Location:................. Germany and Europe
Outcome:................. Trial and imprisonment of RAF members
Casualty figures:....... 100

Huge columns of smoke pour from the wreckage of three multimillion dollar international airlines destroyed by Palestine Liberation Organization guerillas at Dawson's Field in the

1960s–

The Islamic fundamentalist resurgence has been triggered by conflict with Israel and the west, as Muslims search to realize their conundrum of achieving modern nation states where Islam is uncompromised and dominant. These two issues have so far not been successfully reconciled. The Muslim world is not even a single religion let alone a super-state, for it is composed of many races, and just as with the Christian/western world religious and political variations have emerged. When faced with Jewish/western opponents the different terror groups worked toward a common goal and can cooperate; however, they each also have their own private agendas—to increase the sphere of influence of their particular source nation or religion. Iran, Iraq, Libya, Egypt, Syria, Saudi Arabia, the Lebanon, and, above all, Palestine have all contributed and backed their variant groups.

The establishment of the state of Israel in 1948 the beginning of the formation of the Arab terrorist organizations, their raison d'etre to destroy her and reinstate the Palestinians. (A wider aim of more contemporary fundamentalist groups is to unite all Muslims in a new Caliphate and destroy the enemy—western civilization.) The most well-known of these is the Palestinian Liberation Organization (PLO), founded in 1964 with support from the Arab League, with its action wing Al Fateh—originally separate organizations which soon merged. There was also the Popular Front for the Liberation of Palestine (PFLP) which has remained separate but is affiliated.

Jordan desert. The planes, a BOAC VC10, a Swissair passenger airplane and TWA Boeing 707 were hijacked by the PLO during the preceding week.

The PLO has since become the dominant Palestinian national movement, striving for the establishment of a Palestinian state with Jerusalem as its capital. Since 1974 the PLO has been recognized as the "sole and legitimate representative of the Palestinian people" and ever since has represented Palestine at the United Nations and to the rest of the world.

The PLO leadership were Arab intellectuals and their soldiers were drawn from the Palestinian refugee camps in Jordan. They began a high profile campaign of international highjacking—culminating in September 1970 when a multiple hijacking seized the headlines and led to an international incident, followed by war between the Jordanians and the PLO—who were expelled to Lebanon. In 1971, Yasser Arafat, the leader of Al Fateh, became Chairman of the PLO and General Commander of the Palestine Forces. At the same time a PLO splinter group, Black September, was formed to avenge the PLO defeat and keep the struggle extreme. They accomplished this through a vicious campaign that began with hijackings and ended with the Munich Massacre of Israeli athletes. The negative press generated by this event made the quiet disbanding of this particular group necessary.

List of participants:... PFLP, PLO, ANO, Hezbollah, PIJ, Al-Qaeda
Duration:................ 1960s–
Location:................ Middle East
Outcome:................ Ongoing
Casualty figures: .... 10,000+

Soldiers guard the Achille Lauro liner, hijacked by four Palestinian terrorists.

The next one to emerge was the Abu Nidel Organization (ANO) in 1974. It went on to conduct a vicious campaign against almost everyone, from western states, Israeli targets at home and abroad, and moderate Arab leaders as well—even including PLO ones. For the next decade the ANO became the most dangerous of the terrorist groups, operating internationally and murdering hundreds in city bomb attacks, aircraft and ship hijackings, and assassinations. The ANO was eventually forced to relocate to Iraq, where they gave the Iraqis an opportunity to support and sponsor them. A quarrel with Saddam in 1988 caused a further relocation to Libya and Egypt and the ANO faded from the scene.

1987 saw the emergence of Hamas—the Palestinian branch of the pan-Arab Muslim Brotherhood Organization, founded by Hassan El Benna in Egypt and under the spiritual leadership of Sheik Ahmed Yassin. Hamas was and remains intent on escalating the Palestinian struggle into jihad—Holy War, with no compromise whatsoever to be negotiated with Israel. They attack her with every and any means available and make no distinction between soldier and civilian, using assassination, mortar and missile attacks on settlements, and the more recent suicide bombing. As religious extremists they disagree with the more political approach of the PLO and are, therefore, often in doctrinal and sometimes military conflict with them. In 1997 Arafat, in defiance of Israel and the peace process, but in deference to overwhelmingly

popular Palestinian support and in order to save his own skin, had to
acknowledge Hamas and its Islamic Holy War leaders. It remains a highly
influential organization today.

In July 1982 Iran, full of revolutionary religious fervor, sponsored
the formation of the Hezbollah group in Lebanon, to combat the
Israeli presence and create an Iranian-style Islamic Republic there. The
brainchild of Ali Akbar Mohtashemi, the Iranian Ambassador to Syria,
Hezbollah's followers are Shia Muslims and vehemently anti-western
and anti-Israeli. Hezbollah amalgamated with other smaller Shia groups
such as the Hussein Suicide Squad and Dawah to concentrate the Shia
presence and coordinate a campaign that has included kidnapping and
execution of western hostages, suicide attacks on the U.S. Marine and
French military assets in Beirut, as well as extensive operations against
Israel and her Lebanese Christian allies.

A Syrian-backed group—the Palestine Islamic Jihad (PIJ)—originated
in the Gaza Strip during the 1970s, like the others fighting for the
creation of an Islamic Palestinian state and the destruction of Israel
through jihad. Their tactics have included large-scale suicide bombings
against Israeli civilian and military targets and the group is still
operational.

A Palestinian guerilla wearing a mask over his face crosses two daggers at a Hamas rally in Gaza.

The fundamentalist Egyptian group that assassinated President Sadat is called Islamic Jihad, developing from the Muslim Brotherhood, founded in Ismailia in 1930 and spreading to Syria, Palestine, and Sudan. The Islamic Jihad had specialized in assassinating western tourists and Egyptian moderates and has been proscribed by the Egyptian government. It is still operational. The latest and most successful of the Arab terror groups is undoubtedly al-Qaeda, formed in the late 1980s in Saudia Arabia by Osama bin Laden and transplanted to Afghanistan to fight the jihad first of all against Soviet communist westerners and then the U.S. and its allies.

Palestinian leader Yasser Arafat together with Iranian Deputy Premier Ibrahim Yazdi (L) and Seyed Ahmed Khomeini (R), the son of Ayatollah Khomeini, stand in front of the new PLO headquarters in Tehran, which was formerly the Isreali diplomatic mission.

Shiite militiamen fire rocket propelled grenades into Sabra, a Palestinian refugee camp in Beirut, Lebanon. From 1985 to 1988, Palestinian refugee camps in Lebanon suffered from three separated sieges by the Amal movement, a group of Shiites attempting to keep the PLO from rising to power within Lebanon.

*Undated file picture shows notorious
Palestinian terrorist Abu Nidal.*

A PLO soldier sits atop a Soviet T-55 tank overlooking the city of Tripoli. The soldier is scanning the city with binoculars.

Abu Nidal's Fatah Revolutionary Council was considered the most dangerous, active and murderous Palestinian terror organization in the 1980's. This picture shows his followers at the Fatah R.C. Training Camp.

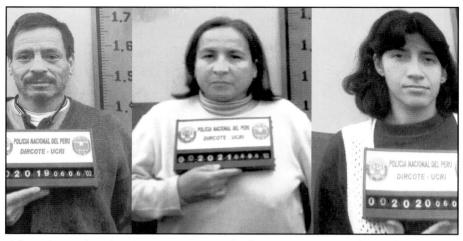

These photos released 12 June 2002 in Lima by the Interior Ministry of Peru shows Roger Torres (L), Lidia Nidia V squez Zevallos (C) and Lucy Margarita Romero Acosta (R), three members of the Shining Path rebel group, believed responsible for the bomb blast that killed 10 near the US embassy in March 2002.

1980–

Two interrelated problems—illegal drugs and insurgency—have constantly afflicted Peruvian stability, it being both a mountainous country and the largest producer of coca in the world. It has suffered from the growth of leftwing communist nationalist independence groups and also organized drug producers. The main anti U.S./government group to emerge was the Sendero Luminoso (SL), or Shining Path, formed as a splinter group from the Communist Party of Peru and founded by Abimael Guzmán at a Maoist university in the southern Andes in the 1960s. This university connection proved helpful for recruitment and for almost the next two decades the SL built up an infrastructure of supporters and guerrilla fighters controlled by a central command.

By 1980 the SL felt ready to progress to armed conflict, launching attacks in the crucial agricultural heartlands of the central Andes, the Upper Huallaga Valley and Puno in the south, in a campaign to cut off supplies to urban areas. True to Mao's principles they began to murder corrupt local government officials in rural areas and assume their functions. However, by destroying food production and farms they also impoverished the very poor they claimed to represent, and in doing so began to alienate the native population. When some peasants cooperated with the government in civil defense actions to preserve their farms, the SL began to terrorize, torture, and execute any who crossed them, forcibly conscripting the young to fill their ranks.

In 1983 a government campaign into the remote areas only succeeded in scattering the SL, who then launched a campaign in the cities in the late 1980s, using car bombings and assassinations. Caught out by this switch of tactics and combined with the growth of violence and corruption generated by the illegal drugs industry, the government declared a state of emergency. The SL replied with its largest single action

Soldiers escort two members of shining path guerrillas arrested in Lima, Peru.

to date with massive car bomb explosions in the financial district of the capital, Lima.

However, a critical event then took place when government forces apprehended the SL's chief, Guzmán. In 1993 he drafted a peace proposal in prison and the SL split into two factions, those against peace led by Oscar Ramirez Durand who continued to opt for armed struggle. When Durand was captured in 1999 it seemed as if the SL was finished. However, it now seems that—as with the Contras and other South American political groups—the SL has become criminalized and increasingly involved in the booming coca industry.

List of participants:... Sendero Luminoso, Peruvian government
Duration:................. 1980–
Location:.................. Peru
Outcome:................. Ongoing
Casualty figures: 30,000

Undated file picture of Alvaro Loiacono, wanted by Italian police in connection with the 1978 assassination of former Italian prime minister Aldo Moro. Loiacono was arrested Friday 02 June 2000 in Corsica.

1970–90

Post-World War II Italy's precarious democracy has suffered from determined and sustained attacks from extreme groups at both ends of the political spectrum, with a sinister Fascist presence much stronger than in other European countries. On the left, one of the most violent to emerge from the student protests and social unrest of the 1960s was the Brigada Rosse (BR), or Red Brigades, founded in 1969. Its terrorist campaign began in 1970 by targeting capitalists with the bombing of factories and the kidnapping of executives. When some of the BR were caught and imprisoned in 1974, the group switched its attack to the state with the abduction of a Genoese magistrate. The BR followed this with the assassination of the state prosecutor, Signor Francesco Coco, in June 1976 and led to a postponement in the trial of captured BR members.

The year of 1977 saw an intense series of attacks on journalists, politicians, and industrialists, characterized by the signature shooting of victims in the legs. This rising tide of anarchy was crowned with the capture of the president of the Italian Christian Democratic Party, Aldo Moro. Prime minister five times between 1963 and 1976 and expected to become the next President of Italy, Moro was seized from his car and his bodyguards killed in Rome in broad daylight. A huge combined operation launched by the police and army failed to find any trace of him, while the BR released bulletins that stated he had been tried and condemned to death unless a deal to exchange him for the release of all BR prisoners was agreed upon. The government refused to negotiate with the BR and Moro's bullet-riddled body was found on May 9 in a car in the center of Rome.

Picture dated 20 April 1978 of former Italian Prime Minister Aldo Moro, after he was kidnapped by far-left Brigate Rosse (Red Brigades) organisation.

For the BR this was a turning point—but not the one they expected. Public opinion now reviled them and a concerted government campaign began to yield consistent results. A NATO general they kidnapped was freed in a daring operation that also cracked open a cell and led to many arrests. The BR retired to regroup and did not resurface until the mid-1980s. Using the same tactics on the same targets they again achieved the opposite of what they supposedly intended—the alienation of the common people at such atrocities. Their actions grew more desultory and by the late 1990s had fizzled out.

List of participants:...Italian government, Brigata Rosse
Duration:..................1970–90
Location:...................Italy
Outcome:..................Marginalization of the extreme RAF
Casualty figures:.......100

ETA attack in center of madrid 10 people were injured when a car bomb exploded in the center of Madrid.

1959–

The Euzkadi Ta Askatasuna (ETA)—Basque Fatherland and Liberty— terrorist group was founded in 1959 by activists dissatisfied with the moderate nationalism of the mainstream Basque party and seeking to establish an independent Basque homeland that would span the border region of northern Spain and southwestern France. ETA's first campaign began that year with bomb attacks in the Spanish cities of Bilbao, Vitoria, and Santander. In 1961 ETA made an unsuccessful attempt to derail a train carrying veterans to an anniversary celebration of the Spanish Civil War, and this aggravated a ferocious response from Franco's police, with road blocks, house searches, arrests, and the widespread use of torture, which resulted in more Basques being recruited into ETA's ranks. In 1973 ETA scored a coup with the assassination of Franco's potential successor, Admiral Luis Carrero Blanco.

When General Franco died in 1976 and democracy was restored to Spain, considerable autonomy was granted to the country's various regions. The Basques were given their own parliament with control over issues such as education and taxes, while the Basque language and culture was promoted in schools. However, for a minority in ETA this partial autonomy was not enough. They believed that Basques should have full independence from Spain, and to this end intensified their campaign— primarily against government officials, the security services and military forces, politicians, and judicial figures. The battleground was the streets of Spanish cities where there have always been collateral civilian casualties—indeed sometimes they were even targeted deliberately as in the case of tourist areas. ETA was also in contact with various other terrorist organizations including the Irish Republican Army and the Palestine Liberation Organization; ETA members received terrorist training in Lebanon, Libya, South Yemen, Nicaragua, and Cuba. The

900,000 people marched through Barcelona streets to protest against the murder of Ernest Lluch, a former Socialist Minister, by the terrorist group ETA.

group financed itself in classic fashion with kidnappings, ransoms, robberies, and extortion.

In 1995 there was an ETA attempt to assassinate King Juan Carlos in Majorca and another aimed at the leader of the Popular Party, Jose Maria Anzar. In 1997 and 1998 they managed to assassinate two other Popular Party members. While ETA had always targeted the Spanish government, its dispute had been interpreted as an internal matter, but with the failed attempt to car bomb the EU-Latin American summit held in Madrid in the new century, they had attacked an international target for the first time. The plot was discovered by the Spanish police who intercepted ETA operatives with over 400lb of explosives. ETA is still operational.

List of participants:... Spanish government, ETA
Duration:................. 1959–
Location:.................. Spain and France
Outcome:................. Ongoing
Casualty figures: 1,000

Red Army militant and Palestinian sympathizer Kozo Okamoto, the only terrorist to survive the suicide attack at Lod Airport on May 30, 1972, stands trial for killing 26 civilians and injuring 78 others. Okamoto served 13 years of a life sentence in solitary confinement in an Israeli prison, but was freed in May 1985 in an exchange of prisoners between Israeli and Palestinian forces.

1970–88

Japanese left wing protest began in the 1950s—primarily against the U.S.-Japan alliance. By the 1960s there were large pitched battles with the police—both sides armed with clubs and sticks, wearing helmets, and carrying banners. The police invariably won. In the early 1970s various elements split off from the Japanese Communist Party, dissatisfied with the level of protest action against the state and wishing to escalate confrontation.

Two particular individual groups eventually joined together to form the Japanese Red Army (JRA). The leaders of these groups—Hiroka Nagata and Tsureo Mori—took their group into the mountains north of Tokyo to undergo training for a suicide mission against the monarchy and the top echelons of government. When some members began to voice doubts about the wisdom of this plan they were tortured and murdered—police later found 14 disfigured bodies buried in the snow. The JRA first hit the headlines with the hijacking of a JAL internal flight to North Korea—a country of refuge and support for their cause. Some of the members then also traveled to Lebanon's anarchic Bekaa valley to make use of the extensive terrorist training facilities installed

Arrest of Fusako Shigenobu, former member of the 'Red Army' organization that was involved in international terrorism during the 1970s, on arrival in Tokyo, having come from Osaka.

there by the PLO. After this, over the next two years, the JRA hit the international scene—literally—with a campaign that included hijackings, embassy and business bombings, and attacks on industrialists. Their most infamous operation, the Lod airport massacre in 1972, was conducted in tandem with Palestinian Arab terrorists. Eventually security operations in Japan forced the relocation of the group to the Lebanon, with a smaller presence in North Korea. Their last known action occurred in 1988 with the bombing of an American service club in Italy, another member being caught in the U.S. trying to launch a simultaneous attack. Since then their numbers have dwindled as they have been hunted down by international agencies.

List of participants:... Japanese government, JRA
Duration:................. 1970–88
Location:.................. Primarily Japan
Outcome:................. Gradual elimination of JRA
Casualty figures:....... 100

The Kurdish rebels mounted a large campaign during the early 1980s against Iran, Iraq, and Turkey in an attempt to regain sovereignty over their homeland.

1925–

The unfortunate Kurds have been manipulated and abused by the countries—Turkey, Iran, and Iraq—who rule the Kurds' ancient homeland of Kurdistan. Beyond the territorial imperative driving these states are the natural resources, especially oil reserves, that occur within their Kurdish areas. When combined with the proximity of larger ethnic populations, this makes the Kurds' struggle doubly difficult. After World War I the Kurds in Turkey were encouraged by the 1920 Treaty of Sèvres which made a provision for an autonomous Kurdish state; however, following the Turkish revival under Ataturk, the 1923 Treaty of Lausanne omitted any mention of a Kurdish nation. The consequent revolts in 1925 and 1930 were savagely and systematically repressed by the Turks, who also proscribed the teaching and speaking of Kurdish. The problem then simmered on until the mid-1980s when the communist Kurdistan Workers Party (PKK) was founded and sustained conflict broke out again in a cycle of guerrilla attacks and government counterinsurgency operations.

The Kurds in Iran also rebelled during the 1920s and were also savagely defeated. After the 1979 revolution and the founding of the Islamic Republic in Iran, any hopes of change were soon shattered when Iranians launched their own murderous campaign against them. In Iraq, too, the Kurds' struggle for autonomy originated in the 1930s and began in earnest the 1960s. It has led to sustained vicious suppression by the Iraqi government.

PKK's General Secretary and military leader Abdullah Ocalan greets women soldiers at the Mahsun Korkmaz Academy military training camp.

Both Iran and Iraq used their Kurdish minorities as a weapon against the other in the 1980s, using the lure of independence to enlist their military support. After the war both countries promptly suppressed the Kurds once again, in Iraq with poison gas attacks on Kurdish villages and the execution of all males—resulting in over 200,000 deaths in 1988 alone. In 1991 there was another uprising coinciding with the first Gulf War, but when Saddam still remained after the conflict he again murderously suppressed them and many fled into the Turkish and Iranian parts of Kurdistan. Following the first Gulf War in 1992 the Kurds established their own autonomous region in northern Iraq, and by 1999 the Democratic Party and the Patriotic Union of Kurdistan reached an agreement to share power. Tribal and political divisions, encouraged and maintained by the larger states in which the Kurds are incorporated, continue to hold back the Kurds' development. Kurdish forces helped the U.S.-led invasion of Iraq in the second Gulf War and seized the traditionally Kurdish cities of Kirkuk and Mosul. Turkey and Iran are alarmed at this course of events. The situation is currently still under development.

List of participants:... PKK, Peshmerga, Iran, Iraq, Turkey
Duration:................. 1925–
Location:................. Kurdistan
Outcome:................. Ongoing
Casualty figures: 500,000–1,000,000

HMS Sir Galahad ablaze after the Argentine air raid on June 8th at Bluff Cove near Fitzroy settlement on East Falkland.

APRIL 2–JUNE 20, 1982

The Falklands were discovered by Britain in 1592, first settled by the French in 1764, then sold to the Spanish in 1767. In 1820 they were then occupied by Argentina—who were expelled by the British in 1833. The British have remained there since and this is the source of the disagreement between the two countries, both of whom would continue to underestimate the strength of feeling on the opponent's side.

By the late 1980s the Argentine military government in classic fashion sought to distract attention from their own incompetence and despotism by resurrecting Argentine claims to the Malvinas—the Argentine name for the islands. On April 2, 1982, Argentine forces invaded and captured the islands and the following day the UN backed the indignant British protests. The Argentines then seized South Georgia on April 4 after a firefight with British marines. On April 5 a task force left the UK bound for the Falklands and a week later the British declared a 200-mile exclusion zone around them. Less than a month later on May 2, the Argentine cruiser Belgrano was sunk by a British submarine and the rest of the ageing Argentine fleet promptly returned to port for the remainder of the hostilities. May 4 saw the British ship Sheffield destroyed by an Exocet missile launched from Argentine Super Etendard fighter. On May 12 the British 5th Infantry Brigade set sail for the Falklands aboard the QE2 liner. On May 21 4,000 British troops make a nocturnal amphibious landing at San Carlos on the northern coast of East Falkland and establish a beach-head. Though the Argentine Navy has vanished the Air Force put up a good fight and sank quite a few British ships—HMS Ardent on the 21st, HMS Antelope on the 23rd, and on the 25th the transport Atlantic Conveyor with its vital cargo of helicopters. Also HMS Coventry, with at least three others, was damaged. The Argentines lost over thirty aircraft carrying out these assaults.

Gurkha troops, dug in on a hillside at san carlos bay, during the falklands conflict.

Meanwhile on land over May 27/28 the British burst out of their San Carlos bridgehead and assaulted Darwin and Goose Green, taking both after fierce fighting. On June 1 the 5,000 extra men of 5 Infantry Brigade landed at San Carlos and there were now sufficient numbers in theater for the British assault on the capital Port Stanley. During this build-up Argentine air assaults accounted for two more ships Sir Galahad and Sir Tristram which had troops on board, some of whom were killed and injured.

List of participants:... Britain, Argentina
Duration:................ April 2–June 20, 1982
Location:................. Falkland Islands
Outcome:................. Argentine expulsion
Casualty figures: 1000

Crewmen swarm around Sea Harriers on the flight deck of the carrier HMS Hermes as she patrols with the British task force off the Falkland Islands.

The Falklands War illustrated the vulnerability of surface ships to anti-ship missiles fired from land or air and it reaffirmed the importance of aircraft in naval warfare—the Harrier VTOL jump jet certainly proved itself an excellent and effective weapons system. On June 11 the British launched a brigade-sized night assault on the critical high ground around Port Stanley, with commandos supported by naval gunfire simultaneously taking Mount Harriet, Two Sisters, and Mount Longdon despite stiff Argentine resistance. Two days later in another night attack, 2nd Para captured Wireless Ridge and the 2nd Scots Guards captured Mount Tumbledown.

On June 14 with the British now overlooking Port Stanley and the Argentine troops bottled up and easy targets, the commander of the Argentine garrison in Port Stanley surrendered his 9800 men. On June 20 the British retook the South Sandwich Islands and declared the hostilities at an end. The war enhanced Britain's world standing and the popularity of the British Prime Minister Margaret Thatcher—ensuring her reelection in 1983. Argentina's President Galtieri was forced to resign, and the military to give way for the restoration of democracy.

Steel helmets abandoned by Argentine armed forces who surrendered at Goose Green to British Falklands Task Force troops.

The might of the Israeli Defence Forces rolled into West Beirut following the assassination of Bashir Gemayel, the Christian Lebanese president, in mid-September 1982.

1982

Israel first briefly invaded southern Lebanon in March 1978, supposedly in response to an attack by PLO commandos on the Israeli coast. In fact incidents had been slowly rising over the years as Lebanon, consisting a mix of both Maronite and other Christians and different kinds of Moslem Arabs, had its neutrality eroded by both sides. With the number of terrorist attacks increasing the Israelis had been planning to invade for some time, determined to destroy the PLO forces using Lebanon as a base with Syrian support. They advanced as far as the Litani river, displacing 250,000 people in the process and ignoring UN resolutions to withdraw. However the success of this operation was doubtful, since the PLO were aware of the Israeli build up prior to the actual assault and escaped northward. It also incensed the Moslem Lebanese, who began to form militias reflecting their religious and tribal affiliations. The most significant of these was the Shi'ite Hezbollah, who would grow into one of the largest and most uncompromising of the Arab terrorist groups, its numbers amply increased by the thousands being driven north into the slums of greater Beirut by the Israeli invasion.

By the time Israel chose to obey the UN and U.S. demands to withdraw, she had created and armed her own Lebanese Christian Army (SLA) to control the buffer strip of land occupied in the south by the invasion. A tit for tat campaign of PLO and Hezbollah rocket attacks and Israeli airstrikes began. By 1982 the Israelis, still trying to finish the job they had started last time—to destroy the PLO in the Lebanon—invaded once again. They pushed as far as Beirut, winning the battle in the countryside, smashing the Syrian airforce and then taking half the Bekaa valley.

Bomb Attack Over West Beirut.

Beirut was a different proposition though, for at that time the Israeli's had no great experience in urban warfare and the Christian militias sensibly declined to join in. After their attacks on the ground were repulsed the Israelis began to systematically bomb areas of the city, provoking an international outcry.

Eventually in August a U.S./UN cease-fire took effect and under this agreement and the supervision of a Multi National Force (MNF) the PLO was allowed to evacuate from the Lebanon—approximately 20,000 left. This was by no means the end of things though, for the Lebanon manifests within its tiny boundaries a microcosm of the larger Middle Eastern problem: it shares a border with Israel and is made up of many different Christian and Moslem factions almost endlessly at war with each other and themselves. The MNF was suicide bombed out of the country for its perceived Christian/Israeli/Western bias by the Moslems. With them gone all the factions then set about their own reprisal massacres and assassinations and betrayals, with the Israelis and Syrians actively participating through proxies. Technically Israel withdrew from the Lebanon in 2000, although until the main antagonists solve their problems and reach a more permanent agreement any pauses in the violence are mere interims.

List of participants:... Israel, Syria, PLO, Hezbollah, Falange, Druze, SLA, Maronite, MNF
Duration:................ invasion—1982–84; occupation—1984–2000
Location:................. Lebanon
Outcome:................. Eventual Israeli withdrawal
Casualty figures: 100,000

United States combat soldiers run in parallel lines across an empty dirt field with their rifles at ready during the United States invasion of the island of Grenada.

OCTOBER 25–MID-DECEMBER 1983

Grenada was discovered by Columbus in 1498, then fought over by the French and British for 300 years, changing hands several times. The British finally won and held it for the next 200 years until 1974 when it was given independence. The government that came to power was the typical corrupt oligarchy of land and business owners, in response to which a socialist group emerged under the name of the New Jewel Movement (NJM), lead by Maurice Bishop. In March 1979 the NJM toppled the government in a bloodless coup and the new government began to cultivate closer links with other communist governments in the region, especially Cuba. When Cuban construction of an airport began alarm bells rang in the Pentagon, for at this time Grenada was seen very much in the wider context of the Cold War.

In June 1983, in a effort to defuse the situation, the Grenadian Prime Minister Maurice Bishop visited Washington, but he was shot shortly after he got back and replaced by his hardline Marxist deputy, Bernard Coard, who became leader of a military government. This was too much for the U.S. and on October 25, under the pretext of being asked in by the Organization of Eastern Caribbean States, over 1,000 U.S. Marines went ashore in the initial assault. They met stiffer resistance than they had anticipated from Grenadian army and Cuban military units and heavy fighting occurred for several days.

United States soldiers sit on top of a tank while citizens of Grenada go about their business below them during the United States invasion of the island of Grenada.

However as other U.S. units arrived and beefed up the invasion force to over 7,000, the defenders either surrendered or fled into the mountains. Beyond a few stragglers to be hunted down the island was soon under U.S. control and by mid-December the situation was deemed stable enough for the troops to return home, leaving a pro-American government in power. The U.S. invasion sent a definite message to Cuba and the USSR that they could not interfere in the Caribbean without provoking an immediate American military response.

List of participants:... U.S., Grenada, Cuba
Duration:................. October 25–mid-December 1983
Location:.................. Grenada
Outcome:.................. Marxist government toppled, Cuban presence eradicated
Casualty figures: 100

ONGOING

The wars fought by nation states against each other take many forms, as do their internal struggles also. Nation states have used illegal drugs to destabilize and undermine other nation states—the British with opium to China for instance. By and large most states seek to control access to drugs by their own populations through legislation. In this way prescription drugs can be legitimized, whether used legitimately or not, and illegal drugs can be fought against—by still further increasing the power of the state. As with political parties that are also proscribed yet continue to exist by reforming under different names or sinking underground, so too with drugs—and indeed all human activities that the state attempts to regulate. Thus the line between legal and illegal blurs. In fact it is not linear at all—but rather something much more ambiguous and interdependent. A dualistic prototype emerges—a ying and yang of legal and illegal, intention and instinct, desire and control of desire. The systematic abuse of legal drugs through commercial pressure is also self evident. "Prohibition ... goes beyond the bounds of reason in that it attempts to control mans' appetite through legislation and makes a crime out of things that are not even crimes"—as President Abraham Lincoln said.

So the seemingly insatiable appetite for illegal drugs by the U.S. citizens themselves fuels both the corruption and dissipation of South American governments, the growth of huge criminal druglord armies and a whole balancing plethora of state anti-drug organizations. Each requires the other to exist for its own continued existence. Political organizations that are criminalized are thrust into collusion with other criminal elements and the interconnection between politics, the legal system, corruption, sex, drugs, illegal weapons and the consequent money laundering is made evident.

Colombia under the threat of the 'Medellin Cartel.

Head of Cali cartel arrested in Bogota.

List of participants:... Drug cartels, drug companies, and governments
Duration:................. Ongoing
Location:.................. International
Outcome:.................. Ongoing
Casualty figures: .... Ongoing

Mexican Attorney General Rafael Macedo de la Concha said that in a Thursday morning raid in Tijuana, police netted several suspected members of the Arellano Felix cartel, including alleged chief enforcer Mario Alberto Rivera.

In the new socio-political tectonic plates of the 21st century some of the previous century's -isms have worn away and as such the left wing soldiery of South America have found it easy to sidestep into the militia of a tribal drug lord. To the poor, cocaine, opium and marijuana are essential cash crops. So all the South American countries to one degree or another are compromised by the insatiable demands of its massive neighbor—despite the attempts of its own government at enforcement. This very much continues to be the case. As the U.S.'s colossal anti-drug agencies fight against the demand of their own population for cocaine and marijuana, a recent U.S. report stated: "we are speaking of a plague that consumes an estimated $75 billion per year of public money, exacts an estimated $70 billion a year from consumers, is responsible for nearly 50 per cent of the million Americans who are today in jail, occupies an estimated 50 per cent of the trial time of our judiciary, and takes the time of 400,000 policemen -- yet a plague for which no cure is at hand, nor in prospect."

Heroin is supplied worldwide primarily from two main heartlands in Asia—Afghanistan and the Golden Triangle in Burma, again with local government collusion—for in reality its their premier cash crop and therefore essential. It also funds the tribes fighting for independence. The most widely used of all illegal drugs—cannabis—has a history of early prohibition first financed by U.S. oil companies appalled at its cheap versatility as source of oil, fiber and paper and then by the U.S. Government because like alcohol, it undermines civil obedience.

Soto Cano Air Base, Honduras -- Airmen teach Honduran soldiers rapelling techniques from a 70-foot tower here recently. The soldiers are part of Joint Task Force Bravo, a 500-person Air Force and Army task force deployed to Honduras. JTF-Bravo has a multifaceted mission of conducting humanitarian and civic assistance, airborne search and rescue missions, and illegal drug interdiction support for the Central American region.

A Palestinian man fires stones from his catapult at Israeli soldiers, during Intifada ('Palestinian uprising') fighting in the West Bank, in Bethlehem.

1987-

The Intifada dates back to 1987 when the Palestinian issue was sidelined at an Arab summit in Baghdad, sparking off spontaneous protests in Gaza and the West Bank. It began with crowds of predominantly children stoning troops, but after Israeli troops killed some of these rioters it progressed to adults with rockets and car bombs and fully-fledged armed resistance, bringing in turn increasingly severe reprisal raids from the Israeli Army.

In the propaganda war the Intifada forced Israel onto the back foot, as television footage of Israeli armored units bulldozing civilian areas and details of the inevitable atrocities began to emerge to a disconcerted outside world. Increasingly, individual Israeli conscripts were also having trouble equating a defense of national borders with the invasion of countries (Lebanon) and refugee camps. This forced a hopeful hiatus—for it coincided with a shift in general geo-politics with the demise of Soviet influence and the isolation of Iraq, with the growth of the Israeli peace movement and strength of U.S. influence to insist on a peace conference.

It took place in Madrid on October 31, 1991. It was historic—the first time Israeli and Palestinian leaders had sat down around the same table. The real negotiations went on secretly in Oslo and led to a peace agreement that was signed in August 1993. This gave self rule to Gaza and the West Bank, and in a further agreement on May 4, 1994, Israel agreed to withdraw from Jericho and the Gaza Strip immediately,

A Palestinian woman throws stones at Israeli soldiers, during Intifada ('Palestinian uprising') fighting in the West Bank, in Bethlehem.

which she did over the next two years. However, the illegal Jewish settlements that were built remained, guarded by troops. Then the peaceful Israeli Prime Minister Yitzhak Rabin who had initiated this dramatically different approach, was assassinated by an Israeli religious extremist.

This marked a turning point, for although Shimon Pires who succeeded Rabin was also of the peace party, Israeli public opinion was swayed by emergence of a new terror weapon that was to have great effect—suicide bombing—to narrowly vote for the right-wing government of Benjamin Netanyahu in elections of spring 1996. Hamas, having had various members assassinated by Mossad, the Israeli secret service, launched these reprisal suicide bombings. The suicide bombing of civilians has outraged world opinion and has a negative effect on the Palestinian cause. Israel is now in the process of building a wall around the Palestinian areas to seal them off completely. The Intifada continues.

List of participants:... Palestinians, Israel
Duration:............... 1987–91 and 1996–
Location:................. West bank, Gaza Strip, Israel
Outcome:................. Ongoing
Casualty figures: .... Over 5000 and ongoing

American armed forces soldiers, wearing camouflage uniforms, patrol the streets of Panama City. United States President George H. W. Bush ordered "Operation Just Cause," during which soldiers invaded Panama in December 1989 to depose Panamanian leader Manuel Noriega.

DECEMBER 1989

Panama's past, present, and future have revolved around its strategic location as the narrowest strip of land between the Pacific and the Atlantic oceans and has been much coveted. First used as a landbridge by the Spanish across which they transported their looted gold to waiting galleons, when their empire receded and Colombia laid claim to the area in 1821 they did not oppose it. In the 1880s the Colombian government came to an agreement with a French consortium for the construction of a canal across Panama's isthmus. Valiant five-year attempt though it was, costing the lives of over 22,000 workers through malaria and yellow fever, it ended in bankruptcy. However, one of the investors then sold the idea to the U.S., despite objections from Columbia. This coincided conveniently with the growth of a Panamanian independence movement, wholeheartedly backed by the U.S. In November 1903 when Panama declared itself independent from Colombia, U.S. troops were already stationed there to protect the new government, which immediately signed over all rights to the canal in return for it being finished. The U.S. threw its massive resources into the task, eradicating the swamps and mosquitoes and then completing the canal by 1914. In doing so it had created one of the world's most important financial and strategic assets and the U.S. was determined to keep possession. In 1921 $25 million was paid to Colombia in return for her revoking all claims on the canal and so it remained until 1968. By then, changes were afoot. The commander of the Panamanian National Guard, Omar Torrijos Herrera, seized control of the government and began his rule as dictator. Although corruption and drug trafficking increased substantially under him, he is revered as a Panamanian hero for negotiating the treaty with the U.S. to hand back the canal to Panama.

Marines of 2nd Light Armored Reconnaissance Battallion prepare to board a C-5 Galaxy at Marine Corps Air Station, Cherry Point, N. C. The C-5 will take them to Howard Air Force Base, Panama, to relieve a Marine security force detatchment at the Camp Hayes compound situated on the shoreline of the Canal, which serves to keep the surrounding area of the base within U.S. control and free of smugglers and intruders.

When Herrera died in 1983, General Manuel Noriega, the secret service chief, inherited the post of Head of Defense. In spite of losing the 1989 elections he appointed himself dictator and remained in power, all the while generating vast wealth from substantially increased drug trafficking, providing a haven for drug cartel fugitives from other governments. The U.S. began to step up the propaganda war against him, and a now-deluded Noriega declared war against the United States. After a U.S. soldier was killed by Panamanians, the U.S. sent 26,000 troops to restore order. Thousands died in fierce fighting that erupted, and Noriega was forced to take refuge in the Vatican Embassy, where he was eventually arrested. He was taken to the U.S. tried, convicted of money laundering, and sentenced to 40 years in prison. In 1994 a new government won on an anti-corruption ticket and on January 1, 2000, the Canal finally became Panamanian.

List of participants:... U.S., Panama
Duration:................ December 1989
Location:................. Panama
Outcome:................. Noriega captured, tried, and imprisoned
Casualty figures: 5,000

Military tanks after downfall of communism, in the capital Bucarest.

DECEMBER 1989

In World War II Romania joined the German side in an attempt to regain territories she had been forced to give up at the end of the previous global conflict. Under the Yalta agreement she then fell under Soviet control, the king abdicated and a communist people's republic was declared in 1947. At this time Nicolae Ceaucescu began to emerge as a high ranking party member of the Romanian Communist Party (PCR), first as the head of the ministry of agriculture, and then serving as deputy minister of the armed forces. He then moved up to the second highest position in the hierarchy under the regime of Gheorghe Gheorghiu-Dej. With Gheorghiu-Dej's death in March 1965 Ceaucescu then became leader of the PCR, and president of the State Council two years later in 1967. He was initially very popular for his nationalist anti-Soviet stance, taking Romania out of the Warsaw Pact and condemning the 1968 Soviet invasion of Czechoslovakia. Somewhat similar to Tito's Yugoslavia, in the 1970s he was the first to negotiate trade agreements with the western European Economic Community, and was one of the few communist buffer states to attend the U.S. 1984 Olympics.

However all this was a veneer, for Ceaucescu refused to introduce any internal reforms. On the contrary using the Securitate—the state police—he maintained an iron hold over all areas of public and private life. A network of spies and informers complemented the state terror regime. In the 1980s he began to indulge in huge over-ambitious building projects which were accompanied by the wholesale destruction of older parts of cities, towns and villages. These were replaced by new style tower blocks into which people were forcibly moved, while he also began constructing a series of ever more elaborate and expensive palaces for himself, while appointing his family into positions of power in the state apparatus.

A man holds a Romanian flag with the Communist symbol torn from its center on a balcony overlooking the tanks, soldiers, and citizens filling Palace Square during the revolution of 1989.

Romania was plunged into debt by these disastrous policies and their repercussions. Riots and demonstrations began to increase. In December 1989 Ceaucescu ordered the police and army to suppress all protests using live ammunition, but the discontent had spread to the military as well. On December 22 open rebellion broke out in the capital Bucharest and the army changed sides and joined the demonstrators. Ceaucescu and his wife fled but were captured a few days later, condemned to death by a military court and on December 25, hurriedly executed by firing squad. A relieved Romania could begin picking up the pieces—Ceaucescu's hideous and inept reign had set the country's development back years.

List of participants:...Romanian public, military, and government
Duration:................December 1989
Location:..................Romania
Outcome:..................Downfall and death of Ceaucescu
Casualty figures: 1,000

Soldiers stand next to debris of an Iraqi Scud Missile that landed on downtown Riyadh, Saudi Arabia.

JANUARY 16–FEBRUARY 27 1991

Kuwait was originally part of the Ottoman empire, as was Iraq—though the two were separate. However, after the end of World War I Kuwait was held by the British and it became an independent monarchy, although never acknowledged by Iraq—who coveted its port facilities and oil fields. After the 1980s Iran-Iraq War, Iraq was heavily indebted to other Arab nations who had supported it and was looking for ways to reduce this load—primarily through the intimidating rhetoric of the president Saddam Hussein. Iraq's small sea access and its port infrastructure was also virtually destroyed in that war and it wanted more coastline for its expanding commercial and military ambitions. By 1990 the border dispute with Kuwait had intensified as Iraqi troops massed and in early August Saddam felt confident enough to invade. The small country was quickly overrun—the Kuwaiti Army just managing to hold on long enough for the air force to escape intact to Saudi Arabia. There was widespread looting of the wealthy emirate, and thousands of civilians and westerners were detained amid the chaos and violence. The invasion was condemned by the UN and the Arab league, both of whom issued demands for a withdrawal.

But the rapid success in Kuwait had brought the Iraqi army to within easy striking distance of Saudi Arabia's valuable oil fields, which rang alarm bells worldwide—especially in the west. Saddam now stepped up his bid for Iraq to be the leading Arab power, for if he took Saudi Arabia he would control most of the world's oil reserves and the two holiest cities of Islam. Using Arab nationalist and Islamic emphasis he argued that the Saudis were in league with the west and unfit to guard the holy shrines.

US Soldiers stand near patriot missile launchers in Saudi Arabia in preparation for Iraqi Scud missiles being launched at Israel.

While his rhetoric escalated, a coalition of forces was assembling in Saudi Arabia, consisting of soldiers from 34 countries: Afghanistan, Argentina, Australia, Bahrain, Bangladesh, Canada, Czechoslovakia, Denmark, Egypt, France, Germany, Greece, Hungary, Honduras, Italy, Kuwait, Morocco, The Netherlands, Niger, Norway, Oman, Pakistan, Poland, Portugal, Qatar, Saudi Arabia, Senegal, South Korea, Spain, Syria, Turkey, the United Arab Emirates, the United Kingdom and the United States itself—supplying three quarters of the 660,000 troops.

On January 16, 1991, one day after the deadline set by the UN resolution, the U.S.-led coalition launched Operation "Desert Storm"—a massive air campaign of over 1,000 sorties a day, using the much trumpeted Precision Guided Munitions (PRM) such as cruise missiles and smart bombs. The Iraqis replied by attacking Israel with a few Scud missiles in an attempt to draw everyone into a wider conflict—which failed. The coalition had instant air superiority and for over a month pounded military formations, installations and the command structure as well as the more general infrastructure of the country. Under this assault the Iraqi army disintegrated and the vaunted Republican Guard was smashed.

List of participants:... U.S.-led coalition, Iraq
Duration:................ January 16–February 27 1991
Location:................ Kuwait, Iraq
Outcome:................ Iraq expelled from Kuwait
Casualty figures:....... 200,000

Oil fields continue to burn in Kuwait behind an abandoned Russian-built Iraqi tank after Operation Desert Storm during the Gulf War.

Burning oil wells, set alight by retreating Iraqi forces, in Kuwait, two weeks after the US-led alliance forced occupying Iraqi troops out of the oil-rich emirate.

On February 24, the land campaign—Operation "Desert Saber"—began, a pincer movement, with one arm striking straight into Iraq, the other curling round to retake Kuwait. The Coalition advance was much swifter than expected, penetrating deep into Iraqi territory, finding little cohesive opposition and collecting thousands of deserting troops. On February 26, a long convoy of Iraqi troops were retreating out of Kuwait, having set fire to the oil fields, when they were caught by Coalition air forces and annihilated. On February 27 President Bush declared that Kuwait had been liberated. The UN resolutions and Coalition agreements had stipulated only Iraq's expulsion from Kuwait, not the removal of Saddam Hussein. Consequently encouraged rebellions by the Shia in the south and the Kurds in the north of Iraq were brutally suppressed. Saddam though shaken and his ambitions thwarted had survived—for the time being.

A long line of vehicles, including an Iraqi Russian-built tank, stand abandoned by fleeing Iraqi troops on the outskirts of Kuwait City.

Soldiers and Kuwaiti citizens laugh and cheer during the celebrations following the liberation of Kuwait City from the Iraqi invasion.

U.S. Army OH-58D Kiowa Warrior helicopters are staged for deployment in Operation Joint Endeavor at Rhein Main Air Base, Germany, on Jan. 3, 1996. The OH-58's will be loaded into Air Force cargo aircraft and deployed to bases in Bosnia and Herzegovina as part of the NATO Implementation Force (IFOR).

1992–95

Yugoslavia's bloody unraveling into its component parts is really only a chapter in a book of history containing similar events, for it lies at the end of Europe and the beginning of Asia and as such is astride the land route of empire and invasion. The ensuing 1990s conflict was the manifestation of deep ethnic and religious hatreds reignited. The three main protagonists were the Serbs led by Slobodan Milosevic, the Croats led by Franco Tujman, and Bosnians led by Alija Izetbegovic.

In 1990 both Slovenia and Croatia had declared independence and had a war to determine their borders, incorporating or excluding the other's majority and minority population areas. Bosnia Herzegovina, with its capital Sarajevo, was the only Yugoslav Republic where no single ethnic group dominated—which made war inevitable.

Slobodan Milosevic and Franjo Tujman met secretly on March 25, 1991, and agreed to divide up Bosnia-Herzogovina between the Serbs and the Croats—and ethnically cleanse it of Muslims in the process. They began by activating their ethnic populations within the country, the Serbian element already the more integrated with its parent Serbia and determined to secede.

Sgt. Henry Drake looks to see where the rounds fired from his M-109A2, 155mm, Self Propelled Howitzer land during a live fire exercise near Glamoc, Bosnia and Herzegovina on May 23, 1996.

In early March 1992 the Bosnian government held a referendum on independence. The Bosnian Croats and Bosnians voted mostly in favor, but the Bosnian Serbs boycotted the whole process. With a 66 percent yes vote the Bosnian parliament continued with the process and declared the Bosnia and Herzegovina Republic's independence on April 5, 1992. The Bosnian Serbs broke away and declared their own state—Republika Srpska—the following day.

Most European countries and the U.S. recognized the independence of Bosnia and Herzegovina and the country was admitted to the United Nations on May 22. Then began one of the bloodiest and most chaotic of post-World War II European conflicts.

List of participants:... Serbia, Croatia, Bosnia Herzegovina
Duration:................. 1992–95
Location:.................. Bosnia Herzegovina
Outcome:................. Bosnian independence insured by NATO
Casualty figures: 300,000

President Bill Clinton shakes hands with soldiers at the Tuzla Air Field, Bosnia and Herzegovina, on Dec. 22, 1997. The president was accompanied by his wife Hillary, their daughter Chelsea, former Senator Bob Dole and his wife Elizabeth, for the holiday visit with the troops in Tuzla.

At first the Bosnians and Bosnian Croats fought together against the Serbs who had the advantage of heavier weaponry and soon gained control of the Serb-populated rural and urban regions, excluding the larger Sarajevo and Mostar. These they surrounded with tanks and artillery and then shelled remorselessly—killing thousands of civilians and destroying much of both places.

In June 1992 the UN brought peacekeeping troops into Bosnia and Herzegovina, to protect Sarajevo International Airport so that aid could to be delivered and from then on their role gradually expanded.

In 1993 matters were made even worse when the Bosnian Croats and Bosnians began fighting over the 30 percent of the country which they held jointly, causing further complications with even more ethnic enclaves, atrocities and bloodshed. In an attempt to protect civilians, the UN created safe havens around a number of towns including Sarajevo, Gorazde, and Srebrenica. In early 1994 four Serbian jets were shot down in the UN-declared no-fly zone and the Vance-Owen peace plan for Bosnia and Herzegovina was introduced. By March the Bosnians and Bosnian Croats signed a peace agreement, creating the Federation of Bosnia and Herzegovina, which left the original two sides again.

Soldiers of the 504th Parachute Infantry Regiment maintain crowd control as residents of Vitina, Kosovo, protest in the streets on Jan. 9, 2000.

In July 1995, supposedly in retaliation for previous Muslim atrocities, Serbian troops under general Ratko Mladic seized control of the UN safe area of Srebrenica and systematically exterminated 7,000 Bosnian Muslim males. The war then dragged on bitterly through most of 1995, with the Bosnian-Croat alliance slowly gaining the initiative and taking much of western Bosnia from the Serbs. Growing outrage at the discovery of the level of atrocities committed made international community pressure Milosevic, Tujman, and Izetbegovic back to the negotiating table. Finally, on November 21, 1995, the war ended with the signing of the Dayton Peace Agreement. This was not an end to the violence in the region for Serbia's premier Slobodan Milosevic then turned his attentions on Kosovo, eventually necessitating NATO involvement and his appearance at the International Court at the Hague in Holland for war crimes including ethnic cleansing.

Members of the U.S. Air Force 86th Airlift Wing load relief supplies for the victims of the U.S. embassy bombings in Nairobi, Kenya, and Dar es Salaam, Tanzania, onto a C-141 Starlifter at Ramstein Air Base, Germany, on Aug. 7, 1998.

POST SEPTEMBER 11, 2001

As the largest and leading country of the west, the U.S. is currently the sole world superpower. As such it attracts the most anti-western antagonism—for it is the largest target. The current shift in geo-politics has seen a Muslim resurgence in the face of western dominance. This is particularly manifested through the continued U.S. support and success of Israel. Much terrorism is directed, therefore, at the United States and its overseas interests, most of it on the basis of ethnic or cultural grievances, but the prime motivator and link is specifically religious and Islamic.

Terrorist groups have found many ways to attack U.S. military and diplomatic facilities abroad. (The most horrific, the massive 9/11 al-Qaeda strike on the U.S. homeland, has its own entry later in the book.) In late June 1996 a fuel tanker exploded near the perimeter of the U.S. King Abdul Aziz Air Base at Dhahran in Saudi Arabia making a crater 35 feet deep and tearing the front from an apartment building, killing 19 Americans and wounding many Saudis and others. The Saudi government later acknowledged that an extreme Saudi group had been exclusively involved. On August 7, 1998, the U.S. embassies in the East African capital cities of Dar es Salaam, Tanzania and Nairobi, Kenya, were attacked in nearly simultaneous suicide truck bomb attacks. The bombings killed 213 people in Nairobi—the more devastating. In Dar es Salaam only 11 died as the truck had been unable to penetrate the perimeter and detonated outside. An estimated 4,000 were injured in the Kenyan capital and 85 in Dar es Salaam. Almost all of the victims were African civilians, but there were several U.S. diplomats and personnel as well.

U.S. and Saudi investigators have began gathering evidence as they investigate the damage to Khobar Towers caused by the explosion of a fuel truck outside the northern fence of the facility on King Abdul Aziz Air Base near Dhahran, Saudi Arabia.

Following the attacks, the United States responded militarily with cruise missile attacks on al-Qaeda bases and training camps in Afghanistan. The Americans also mounted the most extensive overseas criminal investigation in U.S. history to track down the culprits, linking with enforcement agencies around the world. Two suspects for the Nairobi bomb were caught in Pakistan, who when debriefed revealed extensive information about the al-Qaeda network. They were deported to Kenya, and from there to the U.S. to be charged in America. They admitted being trained at camps in Afghanistan connected with Osama bin Laden and stated that the bomb attack was supposed to have been a martyrdom operation.

List of participants:... U.S., terrrorists (mainly Arab)
Duration:................. post September 11, 2001
Location:.................. Global
Outcome:.................. Ongoing
Casualty figures: .... Ongoing

In October 12, 2000, while in the port of Aden, Yemen for a routine fuel stop the American guided missile destroyer U.S.S. Cole suffered severe damage in a suicide bombing by a small boat which crashed into it before exploding and tearing a 40ft gash in the port side. The ship survived as the keel had not been damaged. In November 2002, al-Qaeda struck again in Mombasa, Kenya with a suicide car bomb crashing into an Israeli-owned hotel, killing ten Kenyans and three Israeli tourists. There was also a simultaneous attempt to shoot down an Israeli airliner with shoulder-fired missiles from Mombasa airport.

The attacks continue, along with al-Qaeda's intention of broadening its appeal in the Islamic world. Most recent events include the bombing of a French oil tanker off the coast of Yemen, the shooting of U.S. servicemen in the Persian Gulf, the assassination of an American diplomat in Jordan, and a spate of bombings in the Philippines.

US sailors on deck and damage to the USS Cole after a terrorist attack 12 October.

U.S. and Saudi military personnel survey the damage to Khobar Towers caused by the explosion of a fuel truck outside the northern fence of the facility on King Abdul Aziz Air Base near Dhahran, Saudi Arabia, at 2:55 p.m. EDT, Tuesday, June 25, 1996.

1994-

Tribal Muslim Chechenya was incorporated unwillingly into the Russian Empire in 1859, after fierce resistance. In 1936 the Chechnya-Ingushetia region received autonomous republic status within the Soviet Union. However, during World War II the Soviet government accused the Chechens of cooperating with the Nazis and in punishment Stalin exiled the entire population to Kazakhstan. The depleted Chechens were only allowed to return in 1957 after Stalin's death.

With the disintegration of the USSR Chechenya made a bid for independence, but the Russian federal government refused to recognize the new government and in 1994, having supported a failed coup attempt, invaded thus starting the first Chechen War. Soviet forces initially fared well and overran Grozny in November, but the Chechens had only made a tactical retreat after the bitter battle for the capital and went on to conduct a successful guerrilla campaign from the mountains. The tough tribal Chechens, ferocious and resourceful, were easily a match for young Russian conscripts who didn't want to be there. They also took the war into Russia itself, with a city center bomb campaign that made Russian President Boris Yeltsin declare a unilateral cease-fire in April 1995.

A Russian soldier fires from the heavy machine-gun atop his tank, 14 April, during fights with Chechen rebels near Shali. Russian warplanes pounded several villages in southeastern Chechnya overnight Sunday and early Monday despite a unilateral ceasefire declared by Moscow on March 31.

Desultory negotiations began, but barely two months later Chechen separatists seized a hospital in Budyonnovsk, taking over 1,000 hostages, fighting off Russian attempts to recover it and being allowed to leave after freeing their hostages. This and other similar incidents brought the Russians to a crisis of confidence and in March 1996 they withdrew their forces and more serious negotiation began.

The separatist President Dudayev was killed in a rocket attack that homed in on his mobile phone. With only a fraction of the population voting in new elections, a Chechen President—Maskhadov—was voted in.

List of participants:	... Russia, Chechenya
Duration:	1994–
Location:	Chechenya, Russia
Outcome:	Ongoing
Casualty figures:	100,000

A group of Russian soldiers from Pskov and St. Petersburg OMON special militia detachments hang around on the airfield of Grozny's airport "Severny", seeking a way to leave the Chechen capital 07 Feb. Following orders to leave Chechnya four days ago, this detachment arrived at Grozny airport to find that organizing bodies had obiously forgot about them, leaving them stranded with neither food nor money.

But the country was torn apart with tribal factions fighting for preeminence. By 1999, apparently with finance and logistical help from al-Qaeda, various renegade Chechen groups appeared, raiding into neighboring Ingushetia and Dagestan. There were also more bombs targeting civilians as well as Russian infrastructure. These events encouraged Russia's new prime minister, Vladimir Putin, to reassert central control and send federal forces back over the border. The scale and frequency of Chechen attacks both in Russia and within Chechenya itself then began to climb steadily. In December 2002, two car bombs crashed into the headquarters of Chechnya's federal-backed government in a suicide attack, killing and injuring hundreds. This became a new pattern—the separatists now emphasizing the religious nature of their struggle and showing a connection with events and approaches of other Muslim groups in the Middle East. Suicide bombing by both men and women, became the modus operandi, using cars and trucks for government and army targets. Buses, hospitals, apartment blocks, trains, schools—no place is considered too sensitive; in fact, targets with the most emotional impact are often sought. This is a bitter and uncompromising war full of desperate atrocities on both sides. These kind of attacks, culminating in Beslan in 2004, have if anything turned public opinion against the Chechens and allowed Putin freedom of action. His response is inevitably in keeping with his ex-KGB background. Undoubtedly this struggle for autonomy has become absorbed in the wider struggle between Islam and the west.

Supporters of Chechen rebel leader Jokhar Dudayev, participating in a non-stop rally in Grozny for the withdrawal of Russian Federal troops from Chechnya, stand on the balcony of the destroyed Presidential Palace under the portraits of Jokhar Dudayev and Shamil Basayev, here 07 February.

A Russian soldier takes aim during an exchange of fire in Grozny, 04 March. Russian troops Tuesday pounded the village of Sernovodsk in western Chechnya with mortars, tanks and heavy machine guns from positions on surrounding hills.

El Salvador-President Alvaro Magana (C), flanked by Defense Minister Carlos Eugenio Vides Casanova (L) and Army Chief of Staff Colonel Rafael Flores Lima, reviews troops at a military school ceremony marking Soldier's Day.

1979–91

Having become independent from Spain in 1821, El Salvador managed to fend off larger neighbors and remain so, but with the usual oligarchs in cooperation with the military. From the beginnings of a modern state in the 1930s to the 1970s, authoritarian governments employed political repression with the carrot of limited reform and the stick of the military to maintain their power, despite the trappings of democracy. Finally in the 1972 presidential elections, the opponents of military rule united in a reform movement under Joseapole Duarte, leader of the Christian Democratic Party (PDC). But the elections were fixed and the government remained in power. This led to more direct action and by 1979 there were several communist guerrilla groups at large. Fighting broke out in the cities and the countryside, the beginning of a bitter civil war. The government, in collusion with the military and other shadowy right wing groups, formed death squads who began to kill and terrorize any opposition. The Salvadoran Armed Forces (ESAF) also began a repressive campaign of violence and indiscriminate slaughter in its attempt to eradicate the rebels.

Then in a twist on October 15, 1979, a group of officers and civilian leaders toppled the right-wing government in a coup and formed a revolutionary junta, which the PDC leader Duarte was invited to join in March 1980. Although at first it seemed an improvement with a land reform program and the nationalization of the banks, the junta continued to use the death squads to suppress any opposition, including the assassination of such high profile figures as archbishop Oscar Romero in 1981.

The year 1983 saw the drafting of a new constitution and a realignment of the political scene. The guerrilla groups merged into

El Salvador's U.S.-trained Atlacatl Battalion. The battalion, made up of volunteers and trained by U.S. Green Berets, is said to have seen more action than any other Salvadorean unit.

the Farabundo Martational Liberation Front (FMLN), rejected the new constitution and chose to remain on the outside. The right wing Nationalist Republican Alliance (ARENA, lead by Roberto D'Aubuisson) went into presidential elections against the PDC's Duarte. Duarte won and became the first freely elected president of El Salvador in more than 50 years. Six years later in 1989, ARENA's new leader, Alfredo Cristiani, won the presidential election and under pressure from the U.S. was forced to begin negotiations with the guerrillas. For a few months a series of meetings was held but when they reached impasse, the FMLN began another nationwide campaign of bombings and assassinations. Then in 1990, after requests from a meeting of Central American presidents, the UN was called in to mediate between the two sides and on September 25, 1991, they signed an accord in New York City, creating the Committee for the Consolidation of the Peace (COPAZ), composed of the government, the FMLN, all other political parties, and local leaders of the Catholic Church.

Finally on December 31, 1991, the government and the FMLN signed a peace agreement that was honored by both sides and the civil war was over. By the end of 1992 the last elements of the FMLN's military structure had been dismantled and the group entered the political process as a normal political party.

List of participants:... ESAF, death squads, PDC, FMLN, ARENA
Duration: 1979–91
Location: .... El Salvador
Outcome: .... Peace!
Casualty figures: 75,000

Bombed Out Buildings in Nagorno-Karabakh.

1987–

The conflict between ethnic Armenians and ethnic Azerbaijanis over the enclave of Nagorno-Karabakh (a largely Armenian region of Azerbaijan) has become the longest-running in the former Soviet Union, reflecting both the world's religious problems—the Azeris are Muslim, the Armenians Christian—and also the importance of oil. Only 20 miles away from Nagorno-Karabakh, inside Azerbaijan, runs a vital oil pipeline—part of an $8billion international project.

As the USSR neared collapse, the rival ethnic groups jockeyed for territory. In 1987–88 when 165,000 Azeris were driven out of Armenia, it triggered a massacre of Armenians in the Azerbaijani city of Sumgait in February 1988. By January 1990, Moscow decided it had to send troops to Azerbaijan to quell the violence against Armenians over Nagorno-Karabakh which had broken out in the sensitive and vital oil province of Baku when Azeri refugees from Armenia began another massacre of Armenians. The 200,000 Russian troops brutally suppressed all disturbances and declared a state of emergency.

As the Soviet Union was officially dissolved: Armenia declared itself independent in September 1991; in October Azerbaijan did the same; in December the Armenians in Nagorno-Karabakh declared an independent state, too. Nagorno-Karabakh then became the focus of a full-scale war when Armenian forces from Nagorno-Karabakh, with the support of the Republic of Armenia, conducted a massive military offensive into the enclave, and the following year extended it into the Azeri-populated provinces. The ill-organized Azerbaijani forces were pushed back by the assault but began to fight back tenaciously until a cease-fire was agreed in May 1994. By December the Conference on Security and Cooperation in Europe had decided to dispatch a multinational peacekeeping force

The age-old ethnic struggle between Armenia and Azerbaijan over the region of Artsakh is aggravated at the end of 1989 when the USSR abolishes the Special Administration Committee of Nagorno-Karabakh which was decreed to subordinate the region directly to Moscow. Instead, the Organizational Committee of Nagorno-Karabakh is formed to reinstate the jurisdiction of Azerbaijan, provoking Armenians to declare the reunification of Armenia and Artsakh. On January 28, 1990 Armenian leader Edik Margossian was killed by the the Red Army.

to police the disputed area and in January 1996 the Minsk group was formed, consisting of Russia, Finland, Belarus, France, Germany, Hungary, Italy, Sweden, Turkey, and the United States, tasked with finding a solution to the conflict. In February 1996 an incident on the border brought the 20-month armistice in the Nagorno-Karabakh region to an end, both sides blaming each other for the renewal of military operations.

Today, the issues are still unresolved. They were complicated after 9/11 by the requirement for U.S. to have allies in the area to help in the war against terrorism in general, and al-Qaeda and the Taliban in Afghanistan in particular. All the while, in the background, is the overriding importance of the area's oil: the battle for the Caspian is in full swing.

List of participants:...Armenia, Azerbaijan
Duration:.................1987–
Location: ....Nagorno-Karabakh
Outcome:..................Unresolved
Casualty figures: ....25,000 soldiers

Rwandan soldiers (Background) look at a Zairean soldier as they stand in the no-mansland between Rwanda and Zaire 13 February as they wait for the military equipment that was taken into Zaire by the former Hutu army as they fled into Zaire and became refugees.

SPRING 1994

The most terrible genocide of the late twentieth century took place in Rwanda in April-May 1994. The country had been ruled by the Hutu dictator Habyarimana's one-party regime since 1973.

This had a long history of attacks on the Tutsi minority that forced large numbers of them to flee to neighboring countries. Many exiles fought in Uganda with the National Resistance Army, helping to overthrow the dictatorship of Milton Obote in 1986. In 1990 these exiles formed the Rwandan Patriotic Front (RPF) and invaded their home country to topple the Habyarimana regime. The struggle was vicious and bitter on both sides; thousands of people being displaced in the face of increasing massacres and reprisals. By 1993 the RPF was close to the capital Kigali and only the intervention of French troops to bolster the regime checked its advance. International pressure now forced the Rwandan government to negotiate with the RPF, and eventually the Arusha Accords were worked out and signed, providing for the rule of law, power-sharing, repatriation of refugees, and the integration of the RPF and Rwandese Armed Forces.

However, Habyarimana prevented the Accords from being implemented, establishing instead the Interahamwe militia—the Hutu killing machine that would initiate a campaign of genocide against the Tutsis. Using the pretext of an assassination attempt Habyarimana first eliminated all political opposition, then purged the Press and all institutions of liberal elements. The spring 1994 genocide was meticulously planned and organized, involving people across all levels of society—politicians, army officers, local officials, the police, the Interahamwe, and large numbers of Hutu civilians who were forced to join or volunteered to take part in the massacres. Thousands of Tutsi

A Hutu government soldier in Rwanda.

refugees fled across the borders to other states as a most appalling series of bestial atrocities were encouraged and inflicted. When the killing frenzy stopped, in the chaos that ensued the RWP renewed the civil war and toppled the regime. Over a million Hutus, most of whom participated in the massacres—fled to Zaire, where by 1996 they had combined with the disintegrating Zairean regime in its own civil war, further destabilizing the whole region. The RWP allied with the Congolese opposition led by Laurent Kabila, and with support from Uganda attacked the Goma Hutu refugee camps, forcing them to return to Rwanda, while the Interahamwe militia fled. Kabila's forces then went on to attack and overthrow the Mobutu regime in Zaire. By 1999 the civil war resumed in the renamed Democratic Republic of the Congo. This time the Rwandan and Ugandan governments now supported the anti-Kabila opposition as he in turn followed the path of Mobutu, ruling through increasing corruption and oppression and the support of Zimbabwe and Angola.

The continuing chaos of the Congo and the surrounding countries burns strong, fueled by tribal and ethnic tensions, the disputes over European-imposed borders, and behind it all the hugely valuable resources of diamonds, copper, uranium, that underwrite it all. In Rwanda, the aftermath of the genocide is appalling, the perpetrators and victims living together still unreconciled.

List of participants:... Hutsis, Tutsis, RWP, France, Interahamwe militia
Duration: .... Spring 1994
Location: .... Rwanda
Outcome: .... Intensified civil war
Casualty figures: .... 1,000,000+

The south tower of the World Trade Center is the first to collapse.

As the towers begin to collapse, the entire local vicinity is engulfed in clouds of smoke and debris.

1989

9/11 2001—forever remembered as one of the most shocking days in American history, when armed terrorists hijacked four civilian airliners and used them as suicide bombs to destroy the World Trade Center, damage the Pentagon, and kill some 3,000 people. This devastating attack was accomplished by al-Qaeda—the most successful of the fundamentalist Islamic groups that have set out to fight Israel and the west.

Al-Qaeda was founded in 1989 by Osama bin Laden, a Saudi Arabian from a rich ruling class family, later deeply influenced by the Saudi extreme Muslim Wahabi sect. Having undergone a radical change from a western to a strict Islamic lifestyle, he then set about his mission and began to organize, finance, aid, and affiliate many extremist anti-western groups under the umbrella of his al-Qaeda control structure.

The first action showed ambition—the 1993 targeting of the New York City World Trade Center, an attempt to blow it up that went awry, killing only six, with the perpetrators being caught and imprisoned. As

List of participants:... Al-Qaeda
Duration:................. 1989
Location:................. Global
Outcome:................. Mayhem
Casualty figures:....... 5,000+

View of lower Manhattan, NY as the World Trade Center towers collapse.

things got hot for Bin Laden in Saudi Arabia, he moved on to the Sudan, where his resources helped still further the extreme Muslim government of Hasan Turabi, including the funding of development of the country's infastructure as well as the supply of weapons. Amply funded from many Muslim sources, Bin Laden invests in his projects because he believes in the Islamic cause—with himself leading the jihad as a new Mahdi. From the Sudan Bin Laden inspired an assassination attempt on the Egyptian President Mubarak, and the U.S. and Egypt succeeded in getting UN sanctions imposed on Sudan because of its support of terrorism. The resulting economic damage and unrest made Bin Laden move on to the next jihad hotspot—Afghanistan, where he found an ally in the Taliban and began to build training camps in which Islamic fighters from all over the world could come and train.

In 1996, at the U.S. al-Khobar airbase in Saudi Arabia, a suicide truck bomb was detonated killing 19. Two years later al-Qaeda struck again with the suicide truck bombing of two U.S. embassies in Nairobi and Dar es Salaam killing 214. In retaliation the U.S. launched cruise missiles at the al-Qaeda terrorist training bases that had been set up in

Afghanistan and the Sudan. The CIA identified and disrupted various
al-Qaeda cells in several countries, thwarting various attacks, but the Bin
Laden-inspired Fatwa against the U.S. continued and the end of 2000
saw a suicide boat attack on the U.S. Navy destroyer Cole in the Yemen,
killing 17 and disabling the vessel.

In September 2001 al-Qaeda reached a high watermark, when in a
complicated operation spanning the world it achieved spectacular results.
On September 11 four full passenger airliners were highjacked and flown
as missiles, two into the New York City World Trade Center and one
into the Pentagon in Washington DC, killing about 3,000 people. The
fourth crashed in countryside as the passengers took on the hijackers and
prevented them completing their mission.

By the end of October the United States had "clear and compelling
proof" that Osama bin Laden was behind the 9/11 terrorist attacks
and formed a coalition against terrorism that included the U.S.'s major
ally, Britain. Soon a bombardment of Taliban and al-Qaeda targets in
Afghanistan, began prior to an invasion in support of the Northern
Alliance. Just over a month later the Taliban government was destroyed
and fled into the mountains and into the lawless border territories
of Pakistan. Thoroughly alarmed and upset about the rising spate of

Smoke billowing from the Pentagon, after the highjacked AA77 Boeing crashed into the building at 9.39 A.M.

attacks on U.S. assets and people, the Bush government elected to remain on active defense and went after the next major threat—Iraq's Saddam Hussein. Hussein had tried before to manipulate events to achieve his preeminence and had failed—but he still blustered and threatened—supporting and praising any attacks on the U.S. That same month the al-Qaeda bombings in Bali killed 200 and more bombings against Israeli targets in Kenya showed that al-Qaeda had recovered its operational capability in that country and in East Africa in general. Meanwhile the U.S. worked tirelessly to track down the architects of the 9/11 terror attack on the U.S. homeland. In March 2003 Khalid Shaikh Mohammed, believed to a key planner and top al-Qaeda official, was arrested in Pakistan.

The U.S. and UK led another attack on Iraq to dispose of the swaggering bully and dangerous megalomaniac Saddam. A month later his regime was in ruins and eventually he was found hiding in an improvised bunker. Al-Qaeda had received setbacks that had degraded its operational capability; however, the group was still powerful enough to be able to accomplish a series of car bomb attacks in Riyadh, Saudi Arabia, targeting enclaves of western workers and the oil business. In Istanbul there was a series of bomb attacks aimed at Israeli and British targets but also to punish Muslim Turkey's alliance with the U.S. In 2004 came the terrible multiple train bombings in Madrid which killed over 200 people—punishment for Spain which had been one of only three countries to support the U.S. war against Iraq. Australia, too, was chastised with the bombing of its Jakarta embassy. On the eve of the American elections Bin Laden released a videotape to the Al Jazeera Arab TV news channel with a message for the U.S.—that he was still alive and at war. To date, al-Qaeda has the highest body count of U.S. citizens of all the extreme terrorist groups.

Indonesian police and rescuer workers at the site of a bomb blast in the tourist area of Kuta, Bali 13 October 2002. At least 150 people have been confirmed dead in the huge explosion that destroyed two bars on the Indonesian island of Bali.

Spain had been one of only three countries to support the U.S. war against Iraq. Australia too was chastised with the bombing of its Jakarta embassy. On the eve of the American elections Bin Laden released a videotape to the Al Jazeera Arab TV news channel with a message for the U.S.—that he was still alive and at war. To date, Al-Qaeda has the highest body count of U.S. citizens of all the extreme terrorist groups.

A Tomahawk cruise missile is launched from the USS Philippine Sea (CG 58) in a strike against al Qaeda terrorist training camps and military installations of the Taliban regime in Afghanistan on Oct. 7, 2001.

Ground crew members wave at a B-52H Stratofortress bomber as it taxis for take off on a strike mission against al Qaeda terrorist training camps.

OCTOBER–NOVEMBER 2001

Following 9/11 the U.S. decided on a more proactive policy to counter the growing actuality of Islamic terrorism. The Americans were also determined to hunt down the perpetrators of the attacks on their homeland. Having identified al-Qaeda and Osama Bin Laden as almost certainly the 9/11 culprits and their current location with the Taliban in Afghanistan, they swiftly set about creating the political and logistical effort required to reach them. Worldwide shock at the 9/11 attacks made everyone sympathetic, and the gruesome Taliban endeared themselves to no one in their determination to take Afghanistan back in time a thousand years. So began Operation "Enduring Freedom," featuring a vengeful United States, with support from the UK, Australia and Spain.

Interestingly enough given the experience of the USSR in the mountainous and rugged Afghanistan, the Taliban and al-Qaeda fancied their chances. However, the Soviet war was fought mainly by half-hearted conscripts and with equipment that by modern western standards was from at least a previous generation. The western forces against the Taliban were armed with state of the art equipment, had total air supremacy and battlefield mobility, and were itching to be in battle besides. They also had support in country from the Northern Alliance, consisting of Tajiks and Uzbeki Afghans who had been fighting the Taliban since its inception. The operation began (with U.S. /UK special forces inserted earlier) on Sunday October 7, 2001. To those watching on television, it seemed a light aerial bombing campaign, but it was deadly: it targeted specific keypoints in the command structure of Taliban and al-Qaeda forces. The capital, Kabul, and two other cities, Kandahar and Jalalabad, were struck with PGMs aimed at specific targets—the airport and military nerve-center of the regime along with terrorist training camps. The Northern Alliance was rather disappointed—though not for

B-2 Spirit Bomber droping a B61-11 bomb casing from an undisclosed location. Retaliatory strikes against Afghanistan began 07 October 2001 with US and British forces bombing terrorist camps, air bases and air defense installations in the first stage of its campaign against the Taliban regime for sheltering Saudi-born terror mastermind Osama bin Laden.

An F/A-18C Hornet is prepared for launch from the aircraft carrier USS Carl Vinson (CVN 70) in a strike against al Qaeda terrorist training camps.

long. At the beginning of November, after much careful reconnaissance, the aerial campaign increased in intensity as Taliban and al-Qaeda front lines were systematically pounded with huge 15,000lb "daisy cutter" bombs. Supply lines and vehicles were strafed by AC-130 gunships, their cannons firing thousands of rounds per minute. The original Mohajadin guerrilla tactics that had been so successful against the Soviets had been replaced by more conventional front lines by the Taliban. It was a grave tactical mistake to try to hold ground in a way that made them easily definable targets. Until the Taliban were smashed out of the cities and went into the mountains, they were mercilessly destroyed by modern professional armies in conventional all arms warfare. The air campaign increased in ferocity to such an extent that the Taliban forces began to disintegrate and disperse, and the foreign al-Qaeda fighters took over internal security in the cities.

On November 9 Mazar-I-Sharif fell in four hours after U.S. bombers carpet-bombed Taliban defenders. By November 12 the Taliban had also fled from the capital Kabul. The bombardment of the Tora Bora mountain and cave system—one of the Taliban and al-Qaeda's final refuges—was now stepped up, and the bloody siege of Konduz brought to a successful conclusion again after a massive American bombardment. By the end of November only Kandahar, the movement's birthplace, remained in Taliban hands and the first significant U.S. combat troops had arrived in time for the final assault. By December 6 the Taliban had surrendered Kandahar to the Afghan forces led by the Interim Afghan leader Hamid Karzai. Now only the Tora Bora refuge remained, under continual bombardment. After a brief surrender or die deadline had passed the attack resumed with Operation "Anaconda"—an attempt to cut off the remaining enemy and capture Bin Laden if he was there. By December 14 they cave system had been cleared and the final elements of Taliban, al-Qaeda, and foreign fighter diehards slipped through the net over the nebulous border into Pakistan. In this way Osama bin Laden eluded attempts to capture him, but in their shared fundamentalist ideology and collusion with Bin Laden's forces, the Taliban had unwittingly brought about their own destruction. Currently Afghanistan has held elections and is attempting to build a working democracy. The balance between the different ethnic groups remains delicate.

List of participants:... Al-Qaeda, Taliban, U.S., UK, Spain, Australia
Duration:................. October–November 2001
Location:................. Afghanistan
Outcome:................. Taliban and al-Qaeda driven out of Afghanistan
Casualty figures: 100,000

A general view of the oil refinery of Rmeileh South in the Gulf port of Basra, 650kms south of Baghdad, near the border with Kuwait 02 February 2003. The refinery will be one of the first to be occupied by US troops in case of an invasion of Iraq. Oilfields have become a prime target for US-led forces under a plan seeking to deprive Iraqi President Saddam Hussein from the option of torching Iraq's oil wells if attacked.

MARCH 19–APRIL 15, 2003

The prime reason for the second U.S.-lead Gulf War was to neutralize any weapons of mass destruction (WMD) Saddam Hussein might possess but also to replace both him and his regime. Using his continued delay and duplicity with the UN inspectors searching for WMD America set a deadline for war. The international community was divided on the legitimacy of this invasion and remained so for its duration. However given the political climate of the time following Al-Qaeda's U.S. homeland attacks, combined with others against the West meant that the U.S. was determined to be more proactive in its defense and not wait until Saddam's threats materialized. The Coalition assembled by the Americans to bring about these ends consisted of 250,000 United States, 45,000 British, 2,000 Australian and 200 Polish troops, who entered Iraq primarily through Kuwait, although they also supported (with special forces and commandos) the 50,000 Iraqi Kurdish Peshmerga troops rebelling in the north of the country. In late 2002 the U.S. had begun to change its strategy in its enforcement of the Iraqi "no fly zones," selecting more targets in the southern part of the country in order to disrupt the military command structure and pave the way for the ground forces. In this way by the time of the assault Coalition air supremacy was complete. On March 19, 2003, minutes after the deadline for war had passed, America launched forty Tomahawk cruise missiles and dropped 2,000 pound bombs on government and military buildings and the presidential palaces in Baghdad. The following day the Coalition troops pushed across the Iraqi border from Kuwait and captured the southern port city of Umm Qasr against little opposition. The U.S. Third Division then raced northward toward Baghdad, leaving the British to secure the Faw Peninsula and take Iraq's second-largest city, Basra.

The main road to Kuwait is filled with a steady stream of tanks and other armoured vehicles on their way to the front line.

The speed of the advance was astonishing, the combination of all arms combat teams and air superiority swiftly destroying all opposition. The British reached Basra and surrounded it, but held back a full military assault, determined to avoid as many civilian casualties as possible.

On March 22 the U.S. carried out massive air raids on Baghdad as part of the U.S. "Shock and Awe" campaign to hasten the regime's capitulation, but Iraqi resistance to American forces temporarily increased in Nasiriya where Fedayeen and foreign fighters stiffened the resistance. March 26 saw the biggest battle of the war so far at Najaf, where hundreds of these paramilitary diehards were killed by American forces. Critically, the vital bridges over the Euphrates were captured intact and the breakneck advance continued, reaching the outskirts of Baghdad as the month ended. For the most part the Iraqi Army and Republican Guard deserted the regime and vanished back into the population. Opinion over the war was still very divided at this time, with much vociferous criticism aired at home in the U.S. and UK, and abroad, especially as no WMD had been used or found—although still constantly referred to. By April 5, U.S. forces had entered Baghdad and swiftly made most of it secure, although there was widespread looting in the absence of any civilian authority. The next day Kirkuk fell to Coalition forces and Mosul to the Kurdish Peshmerga. In the ensuing chaos ethnic and religious tensions increased as the different groups jockeyed for position and power.

List of participants:... U.S., UK, Iraq
Duration:................ March 19–April 15, 2003
Location:................. Iraq
Outcome:................ End of Saddam Hussein and his regime
Casualty figures: 100,000

Smoke billows from a building in Saddam Hussein's presidential palace complex hit during a US-led air raid on Baghdad, Sunday 23 March 2003.

A statue of Iraqi President Saddam Hussein falls after it was pulled down by a US Marine vehicle in Baghdad's al-Fardous (paradise) square 09 April 2003. Iraqis began removing symbols of President Saddam Hussein's 24-year grip on power as US tanks rolled into the heart of the Iraqi capital.

An F/A-18C Hornet, assigned to the "Bulls" of Strike Fighter Squadron Three Seven (VFA-37), launches from the flight deck of USS Harry S. Truman (CVN 75) in the Persian Gulf, Dec. 3, 2004.

On April 15 Tikrit, Saddam's hometown and stronghold fell and war was declared officially over. The search began for Saddam and the key members of his regime, using every means available including offering large reward and the famous most-wanted Iraqi playing cards issued to troops. On July 22 Udai and Qusay Hussein were killed in a shootout with U.S. troops. The continued guerilla resistance in Iraq was directed at Coalition forces and any Iraqis seen to be co-operating with them, as well as sabotage against the oil infrastructure. It was concentrated in the most populated area of the Sunni triangle and Baghdad and was waged using mortars and RPGs, suicide bombers and roadside bombs. Finally On Saturday December 13, U.S. troops captured the man who had eluded them for months, in a makeshift bunker on a Tigris farm near the village of Ad-Dawr. An era had ended, though the violence of his regime had bequeathed a cauldron of chaos that would bubble on long after he'd gone. The ethnic, religious and tribal rifts in Iraq still threaten to tear it apart.

A Soldier from 1st Battalion, 9th Infantry Regiment (1/9) kicks in a door during an early morning raid on houses suspected of housing anti-coalition forces Northwest of the town of Ar Ramadi, Iraq, Dec. 9, 2004.

A photo of Saddam Hussein after his capture is shown during a press conference in Baghdad on December 14, 2003. US forces found Saddam, dirty and sporting a greying beard, hiding in a cellar Saturday near his hometown of Tikrit. Until then he had been as elusive as al Qaeda chief Osama bin Laden and Taliban leader Mullah Omar.

An F-16 fighting Falcon receives fuel from a KC-10A Extender with the 908th Expeditionary Aerial Refueling Squadron over Iraq in support of Operation Iraqi Freedom, Dec. 25, 2004.